Praise for

Karen Wright and *The Complete Executive*

"Karen Wright cuts to the chase. No time wasted. She tells you what to do and why to do it, then lays out the road map to get you there. Brilliant!"
—Marcia Conner, co-author of *The New Social Learning*, consultant to some of the world's largest organizations

"A powerful synthesis of the 100 key practices that have fueled the journeys of countless world-class business leaders. Wright's rare ability to see and integrate 'life beyond the office' as a key enabler in professional excellence makes this a must-read. Don't just buy it, live it!"
—Jonathan Fields, author of *Uncertainty*, founder *GoodLifeProject.com*

"One piece at a time or all in one go, this is the holistic must-read manual for any exec who needs to take his or her performance to the next level."
—Mark Bowden, communication coach to the Fortune 500 C-suite and G8 Leaders and author of *Winning Body Language*

"There are many guides to self-improvement on the market, but this is one of the only books I've ever seen that addresses the myriad ways to become a 'complete executive' from an evidence-based perspective. Based on real-world experience, the author has gathered fresh stories and paired them with scientific data to support her 100-point plan to be effective in life and business. If you don't own this book and study it carefully, you will be doing yourself a grave disservice because it has become a must-read for my clients."
—Caroline Adams Miller, MAPP, coach, author of *Creating Your Best Life*

"The key word is 'complete.' Karen's extensive experience working with leaders at all levels has allowed her to craft the best guide to executive success that I've read."
—Gavin Brown, Executive Director, Executive Development, Richard Ivey School of Business

"There are plenty of romanticized theories about what it takes to build and lead a successful start-up, specifically in the digital media space. The truth is, I've worked many aspects of Karen Wright's 10 steps as my leadership journey unfolded. Our company's success is attributed to our dedication to core values and principles. However, my personal pursuit of success as a leader and executive had no playbook. *The Complete Executive* is an exceptional resource that documents the levels of development and dedication being a great CEO requires. There are no shortcuts—and the journey continues."

—Shawn Riegsecker, founder & CEO, Centro

"Karen Wright delivers a fun, compact, and relevant guide for the *everyday executive* to become the *complete executive*. Her refreshing style and practical recommendations keep the reader focused on their day job, while easily improving their leadership skills in real-time. Finally, a can-do book that gives executives a chance to integrate a triple-bottom line approach (work, life, and making a difference in people's lives), bringing leadership standards up to where they need to be in the 21st century. This book is a new starting point for executive transformation and will drive a revolution in North America's boardrooms!"

—David Ahrens, SAP Americas, Competitive and Market Intelligence Executive, Palo Alto, California

"Speaking from years of experience witnessing extraordinary successes (and failures), Karen Wright solidly debunks the myth that a highly successful career and a fulfilling, balanced life are mutually exclusive." —Eric Berlow, PhD, TED Senior Fellow

"Deep down inside, we all know that the executives who focus on thriving across all aspects of their lives perform better than those who act as if their professional life is the sum of their existence. The trick is figuring out *how* to do it. *The Complete Executive* is a phenomenal book that takes the mystery and figuring-it-out aspect out of the picture. Read it and follow Karen Wright's steps to move from a good to a truly extraordinary executive."

—Charlie Gilkey, organizational productivity consultant, speaker, writer

THE
COMPLETE
EXECUTIVE

THE
COMPLETE
EXECUTIVE

THE 10-STEP SYSTEM
for Great Leadership
Performance

KAREN WRIGHT, MCC, CHC

bibliomotion
books + media

First published by Bibliomotion, Inc.
33 Manchester Road
Brookline, MA 02446
Tel: 617-934-2427
www.bibliomotion.com

Printed in the United States of America
ISBN 978-1-937134-24-2

Library of Congress Cataloging-in-Publication Data

Wright, Karen, 1959-
   The complete executive : the 10-step system for great leadership
performance / Karen Wright, MCC, CHC. — 1st ed.
      pages cm
   Includes bibliographical references.
   ISBN 978-1-937134-24-2 (hardcover : alk. paper) —
ISBN 978-1-937134-25-9 (ebook) — ISBN 978-1-937134-26-6
(enhanced ebook)
   1. Leadership—Psychological aspects.   2. Career development.
3. Time management.   I. Title.
   HM1261.W75 2012
   658.4'09—dc23
                        2012029457

To Brendan and Conor, the best coaches in the world.

You are my daily reminders to be my best,
do my best, and never give up.

CONTENTS

FOREWORD

What's Your Score?

I'm an 81.

But only if I fudge the results a little. Only if I lie a little and let myself off the hook.

Only if I strive for good enough rather than for what I'm truly capable of.

If I'm serious with myself, if I really hold myself to the standard I want to be held, then I'm probably lucky to be a 62.

Now I can tick quite a few boxes of *This Is Success*, and I suspect you can too.

And I know I want to go further in the work I do and I suspect you feel the same.

But at this point in your career, it's a fair bet that just adding to your technical knowledge isn't going to be enough.

Nor is it enough (or even possible) to do what you've been doing so far, just a little faster and a little better, and think that's going to make the difference.

What you need to do is answer Karen Wright's call to become a Complete Executive.

Her 10-step, 100-point guide allows you to find and focus on those elements that will lift your game, increase your impact, and ultimately make you more content with the life you have.

Karen is one of the very best executive coaches I know. With this book, she's now willing to help you hold yourself to the same high standard she holds her own senior and successful clients.

Now buying this book or reading it isn't going to be enough. It's not some miracle cure.

But take the test and find out what your score is. Then direct your attention to raising your score, and you'll find you'll move from your current place to become the Complete Executive.

—Michael Bungay Stanier,
Senior Partner at Box of Crayons
(boxofcrayons.biz) and author of *Do More Great Work*

INTRODUCTION

For the past sixteen years I have been an executive coach to senior-level leaders across a wide range of industries—telecom, pharmaceuticals, financial services, retail, manufacturing, professional services, and many others. The relationship between an executive and his coach is privileged, personal, and real—there are no pretenses and few places to hide.

In the deeply candid conversations I've had with these extraordinary people, I have learned much about how they manage to function—or not—in the face of the extreme demands on their time, energy, intellect, and emotional capacity. While their organizational, technical, and educational backgrounds have been different and their personalities and life experiences have ranged widely, the successful ones, the ones who have been able to flourish in their very demanding roles, have had much in common.

The individuals who consistently thrive in the face of the extraordinary expectations of high-level leadership are the ones who have found the optimal combination of habits, practices, and personal discipline that sustains and strengthens them across all dimensions of their lives. A leader who focuses exclusively on the demands of the business without preparing himself personally for the stresses of the role will not succeed—likely at some significant cost to either the business or his life, if not both. But a leader who crafts a life that fully supports his health, stamina, reputation, skills, and relationships will have a much better chance of a long and happy career.

So over the years I have watched, learned, challenged, inquired, and paid careful attention. I've been witness to thrilling accomplishments and devastating setbacks, and I have noticed patterns. Synthesizing what I have learned from these remarkable people, I've devised a model that encompasses the highlights and the common elements. *The Complete Executive* lays out a system for optimized executive performance, designed to help people in demanding roles function at a very high level, based on the principles I have seen very successful, healthy, happy leaders embrace. A holistic approach to the creation and sustainability of leader effectiveness and resilience, the model and its 100-point assessment reflect the best practices of my most extraordinary clients. In this book, I offer my summary of these patterns as a development tool for experienced and emerging leaders alike.

The system is comprehensive but not all-encompassing—there are many habits and practices that could easily have been included, whether as replacements for some items or as additions to the already lengthy list. The assessment, located in the appendix and available online at Karen Wright Coaching (karenwrightcoaching.com), covers the ten major areas of focus I believe are important, and is designed to report scores on three levels—zero if you've never considered the item or have achieved no progress, half a point if you are making progress against that item, and full marks if you're either satisfied with your level of success with that item *or* if you never intend to make that particular habit part of your life. My intent is that you use the assessment as an ongoing development guide—a continuous improvement program, whether you're already at the top or aspiring to get there. Whether you are an emerging or an experienced leader, *The Complete Executive* can provide you with the necessary strong foundation upon which to build a brilliant career.

1

Make Health and Fitness
Your Top Priority

Health is the foundation upon which all successes can be built. Without health, it is impossible to function in all the ways required by top-level leaders, and for that reason Health and Fitness is the first and most important category in the 10-Step Complete Executive system.

Over my sixteen years working with top executive clients, I've seen those who benefit from great fitness and seemingly unlimited energy levels, as well as those who struggle and have to deal with illness and physical challenges. The fact is, the lifestyle of the typical high-performance executive can place extreme strain on your body. Entertaining, evening and weekend events, travel—all pose challenges to maintaining any sort of healthy routine. It seems self-evident that you should take extraordinary care of your body if you are asking extraordinary things of it, yet too often in an otherwise demanding life the practices that support optimum health seem to slip to the bottom of the priority list.

The earlier you start with a comprehensive health-care and fitness discipline, the easier it is to maintain in the face of schedule disruption and temptation. Your routine should include maintenance activities as well as preventive practices to ensure you are staying ahead of potential issues and dealing with things that do come up as early as possible. The goals are resilience and longevity—the physical wherewithal to handle the demands of your role and a long life to accomplish all that you envision.

In this section, we address the core practices that will contribute to a basic level of general health as well as the extraordinary practices that will enable the kind of peak performance to which top-level leaders aspire.

"Taking care of your health and wellness not only keeps you fit but adds to your energy and vitality levels. Treat your health like you do your investments. Get professional advice when necessary, manage it appropriately, and don't take undue risks. People who make their health a priority have more productive hours in a day."
—Darren Ratz, Vice President, Human Resources,
Shoppers Drug Mart (shoppersdrugmart.ca)

1. Disciplined Eating Habits and a Clear Personal Philosophy About Food

I know how to eat (what, when, how much, how often) to fully energize myself and support my long-term health. I am able to resist the temptations and deal with the meal irregularities that occur related to my work schedule and demands.

It makes perfect sense—in order for a body to perform at its absolute best, it must be fueled with the right food in the right amounts at the right intervals. Sounds simple, right? It would be much more so if there were one "right" answer, but then we're not all alike. Joshua Rosenthal, founder of the Institute of Integrative Nutrition, coined a phrase to describe the fact that there is no one set of dietetic rules that can possibly apply to everyone. "Bioindividuality" means that we are all unique systems that have unique needs when it comes to our food intake. The fact is, if you're going to achieve and maintain your best possible energy level you need to fuel your body with the foods it uses best, when it needs them, in the quantities that are most efficient. The best foods for you may not be the best for others, nor are they necessarily the foods that are easiest to prepare or most available. As with any effort, though, if you plan for what you need you can usually stick with a program.

If you aren't clear on how your body responds to different types of foods, try an experiment. Have something different for breakfast every day for a week—oatmeal with dried fruit and nuts one day, eggs another, fruit salad another, and so on—and keep track of how you feel throughout the morning each day. Alternatively, just eat what you'd normally eat over the course of a week but keep track of both your food and your energy levels and moods. You'll soon find that your body responds differently to different inputs, and your food journal will help you understand how to best take care of yourself. Once you've got a sense of what works best, establish a few rules for yourself and stick with them.

2. Daily Activity and Energy Awareness

I break a sweat and/or walk 10,000 steps every day. I know what time of day best suits me for exercise and I plan the rest of my day around it. I make accommodations and adjustments to my routine when my work schedule interferes with my normal exercise practices.

Most executive leadership jobs are sedentary, in spite of the fact that they require intellectual and emotional energy, so your schedule needs to include exercise to keep you healthy and energized. How much and how often? You know what keeps you feeling good and keeps your body healthy, but if you don't have a regular gym or activity routine, a 10,000-steps-a-day program is worth considering. While there are few scientific studies behind the 10,000 steps target, it amounts to something more than an hour's worth of activity, and every one of my most successful clients swears by that hour as necessary to their ability to function at the levels expected. Kim Yost, CEO of Art Van Furniture in Michigan, says that his life operates on a "twenty-three-hour day." The other hour? Exercise, every single day without fail.

The time of day that you exercise matters less than actually doing it, so don't attempt to add workouts to your life based on what other people do or what scientists say. Rather, evaluate the realities of your schedule and your knowledge of your own body clock and plan accordingly. If you aren't sure what time will be best for you, consider that studies have shown that people who exercise consistently are more likely to do it early in the day, when there are fewer distractions and a lower chance of schedule interruptions. Morning exercise raises your heart rate and revs up your metabolism so you're burning more calories early in the day, and it can give you a great feeling of energy that you can carry into work. That said, our bodies exercise best when warm, and our peak body temperature usually occurs in late afternoon, so working out later in the day might be easier physically. Or maybe you've got easy access to activity at lunch—an on-site gym or a racquet club near the office. No matter what you choose, make a commitment to it.

Of course, no matter how committed you are, travel and business obligations can wreak havoc with your schedule, so it's important to have access to a variety of options to keep your body moving on those days when your usual routine gets interrupted. Walking is almost always possible, and stairs are usually available. Keep an exercise band in your briefcase, extra athletic shoes in the car and the office, and exercise videos on your laptop. Check YouTube for videos about exercises to do at your desk and on airplanes. One client, wanting to exercise when he was traveling but loath to carry extra luggage, negotiated with the hotel he usually stays at to store a pair of his running shoes for him between visits. The overall goal is to eliminate barriers and excuses and make sure that getting your daily exercise is as easy as possible.

3. Weight Management

I maintain a healthy weight.

There's no shortage of documentation about the effects of even a small amount of weight gain on overall health—both current and future—not to mention energy. And while many people's judgments about weight, and indeed external appearance, may be unfair, they nevertheless occur; it's important for someone in the spotlight to consider the kind of first impression made by a fit person versus that made by an overweight person. Add to that the sheer amount of energy it takes to carry around extra weight—energy that could be used in running a business—and you've got a compelling case for maintaining a healthy body weight. Then there's the longevity issue—if you've got a lot to get done in your life, you'd better give yourself as much time as possible. All in all, it's best to stay lean. And it doesn't get any easier as you get older, so don't wait.

4. Goals and Metrics

I have goals for my health stats and fitness efforts, and I track against those metrics on a regular and ongoing basis.

Most high achievers don't limit their drive to their careers or businesses. If you're numbers-driven, why not use that to your advantage in all the important areas of your life? I have clients who keep track of their stats not only at the gym but at the doctor's office, and they work to improve those numbers every year. Whether it's a lower blood pressure or heart rate or a higher bench press weight, keeping track lets you know whether you're improving, maintaining, or backsliding. And if you're going to track metrics, why not set up a friendly competition with family members, friends, coworkers, or other members at your gym? Knowing others are chasing you can be excellent motivation to continue with good practices.

"Exercise is easier with a goal. Sign up for 10k runs and charity bike rides and let friends know you have committed. You will automatically do the preparation and stay in shape."

—Gordon Stein, High Tech Executive

5. Hydration and Supplementation

I drink water several times a day and I support my health with vitamins and supplements to ensure I stay vital and fully energized.

While there is a wide range of opinions on just how much water you should drink, it makes sense to replenish it on a regular basis—after all, the body is made up of 75 percent water. Drinking water crowds out cravings for less-healthy beverages, helps you feel full so you're not tempted to snack, and keeps the bodily functions operating well. In addition, drinking water throughout the day can help combat the dehydrating effects of most office and commercial environments. If you don't currently drink much—or any—water over the course of a normal day, try starting with one tall glass first thing in the morning and see if you notice any difference.

Because few of us are living the active, outdoor, organic, naturally fueled lives our bodies were designed for, it's understandable that we'd have gaps in our nutritional intake. "Unless you are ready to leave the city and start growing all your own organic food, the best way to ensure you're meeting your many vitamin and mineral requirements is through supplementation," says Natasha Turner, N.D., best-selling author of *The Hormone Diet*. The fact is, our foods are nutritionally depleted, our bodies are under great stress on an ongoing basis, and we tend to eat on the run when our schedules don't easily accommodate a sit-down meal. So there's there's a good chance you're not nourishing your body to the maximum extent, no matter how well you eat. It's best to consult a naturopath to determine whether there are supplements that can help you be healthier.

6. Cross-Training and Recovery Strategies

I have changed my exercise routine in the past three months and I have at least three different types of exercise that I enjoy and pursue regularly. I warm up before and cool down after exercise.

Our bodies get into ruts. If we maintain the same exercise routine for too long, we start to reap diminishing returns—we get less out of the same effort. In order to ensure you're getting the maximum benefit from your exercise, your body needs change. According to personal trainer Romelo Rodriguez of the Granite Club in Toronto, Canada, "By conditioning different muscle groups and metabolic systems your body will be able to better support the strength and flexibility imbalances created by the repetitive demands of any one particular activity. Cross-training allows for variety in your workout routine, which can help alleviate boredom and prevent stagnant results by continuously challenging the body to surpass what it has already adapted to."

Having several different kinds of exercise you enjoy is a boredom-avoidance strategy, and also increases the chances you'll exercise when your schedule gets disrupted. If you're traveling and there's no gym in the hotel, perhaps you can swim or walk or go for a bike ride or play golf or . . .

No matter what sort of exercise you do, the warm-up and cool-down processes are important. The typical Type A personality will struggle to make time for these important steps— after all, if you're not exercising or working, you're wasting time, right? Warming up and cooling down only get more important as you get older, and they help you get the most out of the exercise routine and prevent injury—you can't afford the downtime or limited mobility that would result. And, in addition to warming up and cooling down, consider adding flexibility exercise such as yoga to your routine—it will pay off in numerous ways.

7. Sleep

I know how much sleep I require in order to function well and I get that amount most nights. I get up early, feeling rested and energized.

"Sleep is interwoven with every facet of daily life. It affects our health and well-being, our moods and behavior, our energy and emotions, our marriages and jobs, our very sanity and happiness," says Dr. Peter Hauri, coauthor of *No More Sleepless Nights*. Without sleep, our bodies do not function well. Our attention span is shortened, our resilience is diminished, and, over an extended period of time, both our physical and mental health can be negatively affected. And, like dietary needs and practices, every individual has different requirements.

Says Dr. Hauri, "Everyone's individual sleep needs vary. In general, most healthy adults are built for sixteen hours of wakefulness and need an average of eight hours of sleep a night. However, some individuals are able to function without sleepiness or drowsiness after as little as six hours of sleep. Others can't perform at their peak unless they've slept ten hours. And, contrary to common myth, the need for sleep doesn't decline with age but the ability to sleep for six to eight hours at one time may be reduced."

Unfortunately, sleep is often interrupted or sacrificed when travel is required, when meetings or business-related social commitments are necessary, or when stress levels are high. Napping is often recommended and applauded as a support to the body's need for sleep, but I have yet to meet the top-level executive who felt like a nap was a good use of time in the middle of the business day, making the right amount of high-quality sleep at night an even higher priority.

One of the biggest detriments to sleep is the fact that your mind has often not fully switched off by the time you're trying to get to bed and you haven't really prepared yourself for restful sleep. According to Dr. Turner, there are several things you can to do facilitate sleep. Arrange your bedroom so it's optimized for sleeping—eliminate all technology and reading material, use low light, have comfortable bedding, and keep the temperature cool. When you're preparing for bed, make sure the room is totally dark, keep a regular bedtime, and sleep naked (to eliminate discomfort from restrictive night clothing). If you're still finding yourself having difficulty, eliminate television and computer activity before bed, clear busy thoughts from your mind by using a list or journal, exercise more than three hours before bedtime, and try a hot bath or sauna a couple of hours before bed.

If you are managing your sleep well, you should find it easy to get up early, which is an important practice of a great many successful people. Most of my top-level clients are in the office an hour or more before the rest of the company starts to trickle in. The CEOs of Starbucks, Unilever, PepsiCo, Disney, Avon, Virgin America, General Motors, and Apple are all known for being early risers. In the quiet hours before everyone else gets into gear, you can engage in goal review, reflective practice, exercise, reading, or any number of other activities that can support your overall success, and by the time the rest of the world shows up you've already accomplished more than many of them will all day.

"By the time most of my staff are coming into the office in the morning, I have risen early, planned my day while I've run 10k, had breakfast, and have been at my desk for over an hour. I get more done before they've had their morning coffee than many people get done all day. By the time they've finished their breakfast muffin, I'm ready for lunch."
—Dean Henrico, Senior Vice President, Risk Management and Loss Prevention, Loblaw Companies Limited (loblaw.com)

---

8. Diagnostics

I have had a physical examination in the last year and am up to date on all key diagnostic tests, including those related to age. I follow all professionally recommended protocols to manage any current and/or chronic conditions I have.

I have observed the most irresponsible behavior in the smartest people. For example, I was hired by an insurance company to work with their chief actuary on his time-management and people-leadership skills. In one of our early sessions he mentioned—casually, as if it was trivial—that he had had a "bad EKG" recently. He seemed surprised when I refused to go further with our official agenda and was confused when I asked him what he was planning to do to address the health issue.

When people are relying on you—not just your family but the people in your organization who count on you for their livelihood—you have a responsibility to stay healthy. None of us wants to confront it, but we're getting older and more susceptible to a wide array of health challenges and issues, the effects of which can, for the most part, be minimized if they're identified early. Your doctor will make recommendations for the specific tests required at various age milestones, but such tests typically include colonoscopy, mammogram (for women), prostate exam (for men), and a bone density scan starting sometime after the age of forty. And those are in addition to annual measures of heart rate, blood pressure, lung capacity, cholesterol, and key hormone levels.

"I don't have time" is the most common excuse, along with "I'm fine, I don't have any issues," but more often than not there's an underlying fear of actually finding something wrong. It's highly unlikely that you'll get bad news, so the benefit is that you can put it out of your mind. But if there is an issue, early diagnosis is always the best assurance of good resolution—you can't treat what you don't know about. And if you do discover a health risk, don't think that your otherwise extraordinary ability to overcome obstacles will necessarily help you. According to Walter Isaacson, Steve Jobs' biographer, the Apple mastermind eventually came to regret the decision he had made years earlier to reject potentially life-saving surgery in favor of alternative treatments like acupuncture, dietary supplements, and juices. Though he ultimately embraced the surgery and sought out cutting-edge experimental methods, they were not enough to save him. Jobs' "magical thinking" may have defined his business brilliance, but it may have been his downfall in his fight against cancer.

If you have a condition that requires a specific diet or medication, you're not helping anyone by trying to pretend it doesn't exist. According to the *Journal of Applied Research in Clinical and Experimental Therapeutics,* noncompliance occurs in anywhere between 50 and 75 percent of all patients who have prescription medications. While it's wise to be cautious and conservative when it comes to pharmacological interventions, if a medication can neutralize or improve a situation, why not accept the reality and follow the required regimen? One doctor I know refers to five words he dreads most: "Maybe it will go away."

9. Support Mechanisms and Equipment

Every item I require in order to function optimally (eyeglasses, orthotics, hearing aids, etc.) is up to date and working well. Everything I need for my exercise activities is functional, up to date, accessible, and clean.

If you need glasses, get some and use them. If your hearing is a problem, get tested and get yourself set up with the appropriate support equipment. There's no glory in not being able to function fully, no matter what your pride might tell you. Better to see and hear everything than look good but know nothing.

When it comes to regular exercise, eliminating excuses is critical. Take the time to fix your bike, put new laces in your shoes, unload the clothing hanging on your home exercise equipment, and charge your iPod—whatever it takes, so when the alarm goes off early in the morning there's nothing in the way of getting up and getting going.

10. Social Support

I have exercise partners, group members, or other accountability and sociability partners specifically related to exercise, and I ask them to call me out if they notice I am faltering in my commitment to exercise.

If you know someone expects you to show up, it's harder to make an excuse. And if others are involved in the same activity, it's more fun, thereby increasing the chances you'll do it, even if it's cold outside or you were up late last night or any of the other excuses I know I've personally used.

Part of successfully sustaining any practice is knowing where your own barriers or hurdles are—the aspect of "just doing it" that is most likely to get in your way. In my own case, when the alarm goes off in the wee hours of the morning, if I sit up there's very little chance I'll lie back down. So "get vertical" is my mantra when I'm tucked into the warm covers. That hurdle is different for everyone. Olympic gold-medalist-swimmer Mark Spitz, when asked about the most difficult aspect of training for him, reportedly responded, "getting in the pool." Once there, he could swim for hours.

If accountability isn't enough, it's been proven that working out in a group is actually healthier for you than working out alone. Research conducted by University of Oxford's Institute of Cognitive and Evolutionary Anthropology found a measured difference in the endorphin levels post-exercise for those who worked out alone versus those who worked out in a group—those who were in the group had higher levels. The endorphin "high" can be part of the appeal of being consistent with an exercise routine.

The Bottom Line

Maintaining a high level of health is critical if you are going to demand extraordinary things of your body and your energy level. Stay on top of the basics, create a plan that supports you, and have alternatives and back-up plans for times when your routine gets upset. Establish daily disciplines and a schedule of maintenance and proactive practices, and put them all on your calendar. Enroll supporters and experts wherever you need to in order to increase your fun, your accountability, and your access to the kind of assistance that will keep you healthy, safe, and strong. Remember, health is the foundation upon which the rest of your success can be built!

2

Craft a Life Plan

Having a life plan means having a better chance of living a full, balanced, well-rounded life full of the things that interest you and make you happy. After all, why leave the most important things to chance? It's worth setting some goals to ensure you achieve the things that are important to you. Having an overall sense of direction, if not a detailed plan, for your life is another of the foundational components of The Complete Executive system.

A life plan doesn't have to have specific milestones and dates—although if that works for you, it certainly can. The most important thing about a life plan is that it provides a compass or a set of guideposts that helps you make decisions and navigate murky situations in all the major categories of your life. If you look at a "life plan" as a decision template or a thematic backdrop to your path rather than as spreadsheets and lists, it doesn't seem so arduous a task to create one. And since it's about your life, feel free to create it in whatever form works for you. As an example, a senior corporate communications executive and her artist husband undertook a tangible expression of their shared life plan in the form of a piece of art that they created together. It was abstract, but it represented their important goals and areas of focus, and, displayed in their living room, it served as a constant reminder.

Following are some conversations and "think-abouts" that can make navigating your course clearer and easier—for you and for your loved ones. Even if they don't make it into the artwork on the living room wall, discussions on these topics will help you ensure you're being consistent with what you know is important.

11. Goal Alignment with Partner

My spouse/life partner and I have discussed our individual and shared long-term goals. We know where we're going and how to get there together.

A client confided that she was concerned that she and her husband were on different wavelengths about their future. He was a CEO who was close to retirement; she, however, was a few years younger and was still engaged in and enjoying her career. More importantly, she was also involved in several charitable organizations and felt she was making an important contribution to some causes she believed in strongly. She was nervous that her husband was going to want to shift their lives into retirement mode, and she wasn't ready to do that. Sadly, they hadn't talked about their respective goals and interests—he had assumed she'd be ready and willing to change when he retired, and she assumed he'd noticed her continued ambition and her charitable work and understood how important they both were to her.

In order to have a conversation about your long-term goals as a couple, you and your partner need to have both done some thinking about your individual aspirations. It's best to do the first reflection separately, preventing the possibility of agreeing on something just because your partner raised it. I suggest using the Wheel of Life tool as the basis for this discussion (you can find a more in-depth exploration and the graphic in *Co-Active Coaching* by Karen Kimsey-House, Henry Kimsey House, and Phillip Sandahl). A tool originated by the Coaches Training Institute, the Wheel of Life is simple and comprehensive enough to form the productive basis of conversation about the major categories that comprise most people's lives.

12. Financial Plan

I have calculated my long-term financial requirements and I am living based on a plan to meet those requirements.

A C-level client underwent a very sophisticated executive medical assessment. His summary of what he learned? "I'm going to outlive my financial plan." While I laughed in the moment, two things occurred to me. First, he had a financial plan that was based on an estimated life span—fantastic. I don't know enough people who do that. Secondly, his estimate was apparently incorrect, and he now had cause to worry. The good news is that he intended to adjust his plan and his behavior to the new data, to ensure he would be able to finance a lengthy retirement.

Even the most seemingly modest life plans have price tags. Another client, a teacher, took early retirement in his mid-fifties with the intent of golfing as much as possible, all year round. He and his wife had no mortgage and their kids were off leading their own lives, so their living costs were quite low. But he quickly came to realize that "just golfing," when it leapt from once or twice a week to five or six times a week, was going to cost more than he and his wife had calculated. It seems obvious, but given that they had no lofty plans to purchase vacation real estate or travel the world, they hadn't been at all concerned. After about six months of spending at a higher rate than they'd planned, they recalibrated and adjusted their plans, taking on substitute teaching jobs for a few years more until they built up their greens fees fund.

While no test can predict the duration of a life with 100 percent accuracy, there are readily available actuarial tables that can give you a good estimate of your life expectancy, barring unforeseen occurrences. And if you go to RealAge (real age.com) you can get an estimate of how your current lifestyle is impacting your body—are you physically older or younger than your chronological age? Once you've arrived at a reasonable expected life span, you can determine how much money you'll need to live in your desired lifestyle until then. And while this can be a sobering exercise, it's better to do it and know and plan, rather than ignore it altogether and hope for the best. Remember, hope is not a strategy.

13. Career Goal

I know what I want to achieve in my career and I have a plan to accomplish my goals.

It has been intriguing to me, over the years, to learn how many senior executives have had careers that occurred completely opportunistically. In those cases, I am not surprised when the executives come to the realization that they have not achieved what they had thought they might, or that they are not feeling fulfilled in spite of having accomplished great things by conventional measures.

On the other end of the spectrum are those who plan and plot and predict their career paths, only to find out that what they thought they wanted didn't end up satisfying them, resulting in a sense of dissonance or conflict. These executives adhered blindly to a plan that was no longer relevant or that wasn't flexible enough in the first place. Of course, there are examples of those who plan and have their careers work out perfectly, as well as those who don't plan and have their paths work out equally well. The lesson for career goals is, I think, the same as for the overall life plan—you should at least have a set of general guidelines and a sense of what's important but allow for regular reviews and flexibility when interesting opportunities arise. Equally important is to know what will *not* work—being able to quickly say "no" to something is a liberating feeling that reduces stress and saves a lot of time and emotional energy.

14. Mentors and Coaches

I have people I can—and do—turn to for advice and support.

First, let's note the difference between a mentor and a coach, because they are different, and yet both can play a valuable role in your life. A mentor is someone who's got experience you can learn from and who's willing to share the learning she acquired through that experience. A coach, on the other hand, is someone who sees potential in you and can motivate you to stretch yourself to achieve more than you thought possible.

Anyone who's ever had a mentor can attest to the incredible value of being able to learn from someone who has "been there, done that." Mentors are usually thought of as being career-related, but it's just as valuable to have a mentor for your life. The first step in finding a mentor is being open-minded about the possibility that, no matter where you are in your career and your life, there might be value in surrounding yourself with wisdom and experience. Being willing to ask for the support is the next step. You'll likely be surprised at the positive response—most people are flattered if they think someone believes they have wisdom worth sharing.

A coach is someone who listens, who believes in you, and who, while not necessarily having walked the same path that you're on, can see that you are capable of achieving great things and has tools and skills to help you dig deep and push yourself. A great boss will have coaching skills, so you might be lucky enough in your career to work for bosses who coach well, but you might have other coaches who support you and motivate you and stretch you as well. Being coachable means being open to being challenged, to trying new ideas, and to being held accountable for commitments to action, all of which can propel you forward more quickly than you would move without the support.

Both mentors and coaches can be incredibly valuable resources, personally and professionally, as long as you are open to the advice and support.

"My executive coach, with whom I have been working for nearly a decade, has provided me with important, professionally life-altering insights in part because he asks questions of me that I would never have asked myself, and he demands hard answers. Like any coach/athlete relationship, it's not always fun and the athlete only gets out of it as much as he or she is willing to put in."
—Geoff Roberts, Headmaster, Crescent School
(crescentschool.org)

---

15. Retirement Lifestyle Vision

I have thought about how I want to be living my life ten, twenty, and thirty years from now, and I have a plan for achieving that vision.

Do you have a "bucket list"? Are there places you want to travel, experiences you want to enjoy? Have you gotten out your calculator and added up the costs of all the things you want to do? Sit down with your spouse and talk about how you want to be living "later." Will you stay in your current house or change residences? Will a geographical change be part of the plan? Travel? New hobbies or interests? How will you spend your days? You don't have to know all the answers right now, but it's best to start the conversation. Besides, it can be fun to sit down in a relaxed atmosphere and ponder what the future will look like. It's best to start talking about it early, to increase the chances you will be able to live the way you want to, rather than the way you've ended up doing because you didn't think about it in any detail.

16. Social Service/Contribution

I know which causes and issues are important to me and I make contributions of money and/or time to organizations that support those causes and issues.

While there are many worthy causes and organizations in the world, there are probably only a few that you really care about. Perhaps you have personal experience with a health issue or an injustice. Perhaps you believe strongly in a particular solution to a global problem. Maybe you care about animals or the environment. In the throes of career focus and rapid advancement it's often difficult to do anything other than give money, but donating to a cause is a great start. In the later stages of your career, when time demands may be tapering a little, you may want to contribute your own energy and skills toward solving a problem or advancing a cause.

Board memberships are often a great way to stay connected to a business community, keep your network growing and thriving, and keep your brain engaged. For some, though, board involvement isn't "hands-on" enough. Bear in mind your natural interests and skills, and ensure there's a good match between what you enjoy doing and the requirements of the volunteer effort you undertake.

17. Legacy/Significance

I know the impact I want to have on the world or my chosen segment of it, and my career and personal plans will support me in creating that impact.

The typical arc of life features conventional metrics of accomplishment throughout the rising stages of career and family. At some point, however, I have seen many successful individuals approach an inflection point—a "fulfillment crisis," as I've come to call it—where success in its external forms declines in meaning and "significance" becomes important. It's difficult to be in service to others when you are still chasing your own measures of success, but once you've met your own goals, it often becomes apparent that individual success is not quite enough.

Considering the lasting impact your life will have is an important exercise to undertake. When I am working with a client in this area we spend a great deal of time discussing the issues and people she wants to affect, and what the desired scale of impact might be. Not everyone needs to change the world, but it is useful and important to define where you want your "significance" to be directed. A useful exercise I often have clients do is to envision that they are the subject of a future grandchild's elementary school speech. What would the child say? What have you accomplished that would be worthy of the admiration of future generations?

18. Residence/Geography

I live in a part of the world that I enjoy and my home provides me with the necessary peace and restful sanctuary.

We all have choices. Every aspect of your personal environment either nourishes you or is an energy drain. If there's anything about your house that causes you annoyance or frustration, it is sapping valuable energy each and every day. Make a list and, one by one, handle the things that need handling.

Geography seems like a tougher issue to fix if it's a problem, but it depends how big a problem it really is. If you are very unhappy with the area where you live and this is causing you significant unhappiness or stress, consider making a plan to move. However, if the benefits of staying where you are clearly outweigh the downside, then put the negativity away. You can make a change if you want to—you just have to figure out how much you want to. Then you can either take action or let the frustration go, so it's no longer a barrier to your contentment with where you are.

19. Perfect Days

My days energize me and provide opportunities for me to work in "flow."

Mihaly Csikszentmihalyi describes "flow" as a state that requires all of a person's skills in effortless concentration focused on achieving a goal or solving a problem that is just within the bounds of the possible. The sense of complete immersion, of time passing quickly, of being energized no matter what the physical or mental task involves—these are all indicative of a state of flow. Your perfect work—and life—will offer you opportunities to be in flow, using your best skills and doing things you love to do, resulting in exhilarating energy levels and great results.

In his book *Authentic Happiness*, Dr. Martin Seligman, the founding father of positive psychology, introduced the idea of "Signature Strengths." The twenty-four strengths identified included things like "Love of Learning," "Appreciation of Beauty," "Zest," "Gratitude," and "Perseverance." His research proved that actively using your strengths daily leads to satisfaction, fulfillment, and the feeling of living a meaningful life.

Your ideal role—and life—will give you the opportunity to do a lot of what you're good at and allow you to surround yourself with people who are good at the other things. Not that you shouldn't stretch and grow and learn new things—by all means, you should. But if your typical day requires that you spend much time doing things you aren't good at or don't enjoy, chances are you'll experience an ongoing sense of conflict or dissatisfaction that could be avoided.

20. Will and Bequests

My will and power of attorney documents are up to date and include bequests to charitable or cause-based organizations that do work I believe in.

One of the most surprising moments I've had in my coaching career came during a conversation with a prominent lawyer who admitted that he did not have a will. The moment offered me a rather humbling opportunity to learn how to manage my reaction to news like that, but that's a story for another day.

According to Forbes.com, approximately 65 percent of Americans do not have a will specifying the distribution of their assets when they die. The reasons range from a discomfort with the idea of discussing death to a fear of expense and paperwork to a misguided belief that, with minimal assets and no dependents, a will is not necessary.

The fact is, no matter how old you are, no matter whether you have dozens of dependents or none, it's a basic adult responsibility and a legal necessity to have a will. Not having one can be a huge headache for whomever you are leaving behind. In addition, you miss a chance to support causes or organizations you believe in that might benefit from whatever assets you have available to distribute. Research conducted by CDS Global discovered that only 7 percent of Americans specify a bequest in their will, a huge missed opportunity for meaningful contribution and legacy.

Creating a will doesn't have to be complicated or expensive. The toughest part is confronting the idea that you will die someday. Once you confront your own mortality and engage in the conversation with your spouse or partner about how to arrange things, though, you'll feel a sense of relief.

The Bottom Line

If you are determined to achieve something specific in your life, it's almost certain that you'll do it more easily if you have a plan. In the spirit of the old carpenter's adage, "measure twice, cut once," having a plan will increase your chances of living a life that fulfills you and supports you in accomplishing your most important dreams.

3

Invest in Relationships

Relationships, and the ability to build and maintain them, can make or break a career and a life, so this category ranks high in importance in *The Complete Executive*. In my experience, there's not usually too much difference between a person's relationship skills and behavior at work and in his personal life. Someone who fully engages in building positive relationships at work probably places similar value on them outside the office. Similarly, if an individual is difficult to get along with or get to know at work, she is likely the same in her personal relationships. Hence, the ability to build and sustain relationships across all aspects of your life is an important component of this success model.

As I was developing this system and discussing it with clients and colleagues, one person asked me the difference between "network" and "relationships." I have identified and addressed the two separately because I believe they are very different, though related and occasionally overlapping. Both have tremendous value and importance in the life of the successful executive. Both grow strong with time and attention. Given a choice, or if I had to rank them, relationships would supersede network. You can have great relationships that are part of a useful business network, but I don't believe you can have a strong business network if you don't know how to build and maintain relationships. Not that you need to have close personal relationships with everyone in your network in order for it to be useful and valuable—you don't, but when having a relationship is important, you better know how to build one.

So, yes, there are people in your professional network with whom you'll find it valuable to maintain a good relationship. Even more importantly, though, strong personal relationships can provide a solid foundation upon which you can build your professional successes. Having people with whom you can be yourself and with whom you can talk openly and honestly is very important.

Your behavior in relationships can—and often does—transcend boundaries and can affect your professional reputation, for better or for worse. Take the C-level individual who treated his former wife badly in their divorce as he moved on to a younger model: even though the drama and the affected person were in his personal life, word got out and his professional reputation was tarnished.

21. Primary Relationship

I have a life partner and we are both happy in our relationship OR we are actively involved in a process to strengthen our relationship OR I am single and happy.

Love is complicated. That said, most of us would rather live with it than without it. Those who have a great primary relationship attribute to it their sanity, their peace of mind, their ability to focus, and their assuredness that they won't take themselves too seriously. In addition, like it or not, there are still many boardrooms where the evaluations of candidates for the next executive role include a discussion of whether or not the individual has a "stable" personal life—that stability is still used as a proxy for the personal maturity and reliability required in senior leadership roles.

A spouse can be an incredible source of professional support in many ways. I was invited to a party at the home of the CEO of a very large global telecommunications company. As guests arrived, the CEO's wife greeted them by name and introduced them to other people with whom she knew they would have some points of connection. Over the course of the evening, this woman navigated the room, drawing guests in and out of conversation with her husband and redirecting them toward other guests. Her performance was seamless and masterful. Her husband got to speak briefly with everyone and at length with a few key people, and he never once had to worry about whether he'd gotten someone's name right. No surprise that, when asked over the years about his secrets of success, his wife was at the top of the list.

But while a great relationship and a supportive spouse can be hugely valuable both personally and professionally, the intention behind this criterion is not to imply that you must be tucked in behind a white picket fence before you're C-suite material. Rather, your happiness and stability are the important considerations. Single and happy is better than married and miserable.

While many studies over the years have asserted that married people live longer than single ones, Bella DePaulo debunked many of those findings in her book *Singled Out: How Singles Are Stereotyped, Stigmatized, and Ignored, and Still Live Happily Ever After.* DePaulo found that people who were married and those who had always been single were equally healthy. It was those who were cohabitating, separated, divorced, or widowed who were significantly less well. In response to claims that married people live longer, she points to a study that started in 1921 and tracked 1,528 people throughout their lives, beginning when they were eleven. Those who either stayed single or stayed married lived the longest. Divorcees and widows had shorter lives. "What mattered was consistency," she writes, "not marriage."

22. Children

I am happy with, and make regular investments in, my relationships with my children OR I have no children and accept that status.

Having children is usually a choice, so the inclusion of this item is not intended as a judgment based on whether or not you have any. If you do not and you're comfortable with that status (whether it's just not happened yet, it's a conscious choice, or it's something you've not chosen but you've accepted), I consider that a happy state. The intent here is to ensure that your status as a parent—or not—isn't weighing on you to a degree that it detracts from your ability to lead.

If you do have children, you can attest to the fact that parent-child relationships go through good times and bad, and at times are incredibly difficult and conflicted. No matter their age, children can be sources of great joy as well as the basis of tremendous frustration and sadness. If you allow a conflict to extend over time, it can be an enormous drain of emotional energy that takes its toll elsewhere in your life, including at work. So the message here is to work hard at even the most fractious of relationships, so that they are as good as they possibly can be.

23. Extended Family

I have amicable relationships with my extended family and have no bad blood or unfinished business to clean up.

You can't choose your family, and sometimes family relationships get irreparably damaged. If that is the case for you, it's critical that you let go—that you do whatever personal work you have to do in order to be at peace with the realities of your family relationships. But family can also be a great source of happiness and positive energy, so it's worth investing in your family relationships to create them as positively as possible.

If you have great relationships with your extended family members, be sure to take the time to enjoy them regularly, because connections with the people who love you and know you best can be wonderful infusions of positive fuel.

On the other hand, if you have conflicted relationships, taking the time to clean up any lingering issues with members of your extended family can be remarkably invigorating. It requires a lot of courage to address something that may have been festering for a long while, but anyone who does it admits that it was worth it. Removing an energy drain or emotional sore spot makes you feel lighter and freer.

Depending on the size of your family and family members' own networks and interests, family can have an impact on your business. I have a relative who has his own incredible network, and we have often provided each other with valuable connections.

24. Neighbors

I know my neighbors by name and have chatted with some of them recently.

Show me a bad neighbor and I'll show you someone who's difficult to work for. How we show up in our off hours is a reflection of who we are as people. Saying "good morning"—or not—when you're taking out the garbage or reaching for the morning paper may be the only moment of contact you have with those next-door neighbors. If that's all the data you're giving them, they'll form an opinion based on it, whether it's accurate or not. Take a moment to chat, shovel the elderly neighbor's walk, say hi to the kids next door—it's all small and it all counts.

The individual who's pleasant to chat with and who cares enough to remember the names of the neighbor's grandkids and that the teenager across the street just went off to university, that's a decent human being who has a heart and brings that heart with him to the office every day. And don't underestimate the potential impact of your neighbors' opinions on your professional world. On my street there are several neighbors who are one degree of separation from some of my biggest clients. Burn no bridges...

25. Community

I feel like I am part of a community outside of work.

To rely exclusively on professional colleagues for a social life is to open the door to potential complications, not to mention putting all one's social eggs in one basket. Belonging to a group or community gives us a sense of identity. It helps us understand who we are and lets us feel a part of something larger than ourselves. Researchers also find that people with strong social connections have less stress-related health problems, lower risk of mental illness, and faster recovery from trauma or illness.

Some people find community based on their religion or faith, others make connections based on sports, others are active in their neighborhoods, and still others volunteer at their children's schools. Where and with whom you find community is not important—being involved and connected is the goal.

26. Competitors

I have amicable professional relationships with key players at my major competitors.

Walking the high road is something that can earn you tremendous respect. In many industries there are reasons for competitors to find themselves in the same place at the same time, and your image can be improved or diminished based on your behavior in those potentially charged situations. In addition, there are often issues that affect entire industries or economic sectors that require conversation and collaboration to resolve, and if you've got collegial relationships with competitors you'll be equipped to participate in those discussions.

"I do all things with the perspective that 'the road is long and the world is small.' Leave a good impression in every interaction. Today's 'adversary' is potentially tomorrow's valued client or reference. Seeking win/win sounds altruistic, but it's very pragmatic."
—David Wright, CEO, Agora Consulting Partners
(agorainc.com)

---

27. Peers

I have same-level friends and colleagues and regularly invest in my relationships with them.

Marcus Buckingham and Donald O. Clifton of the Gallup organization wrote, in their classic book *Now Discover Your Strengths,* that there are twelve things that everyone needs at work, and one of them is a "best friend." In their view, because work is a social experience, the ability to develop trusting relationships with coworkers is a key component of what they call "emotional compensation" and company loyalty. As a leader, it is important to ensure you are creating a work environment where employees believe they can trust their coworkers. Your ability to do that depends in part on the way you are modeling the role for your organization—whether you've got your own peer relationships.

In my coaching work, when I assess leadership competencies I often find that the ability to build peer relationships is under-developed. Leaders find it easy to understand that they must invest in relationships with their direct reports—after all, they are the ones who do the work. Investing upward makes good career sense—building relationships with executives further up the hierarchy can pay dividends when it comes to promotions and special opportunities. Relationships with peers, however, often fall to the bottom of the priority list, whether it's because the value is not as clear or because peers are perceived as competitors. Whatever the reason, you're missing some valuable connections if you're not investing with your peers.

If you are the top-level leader in your organization, though, you may not have same-level peers or colleagues, at least none that are immediately evident. In that case, you need to cast your net a little wider than your own company. Organizations like your local Board of Trade, the Young Presidents' Organization, or the local Rotary Club are often great places to meet people of similar experience and responsibility levels with whom you can build friendships.

One very practical consideration when it comes to peer relationships is the fact that if you aspire to greater responsibility you might have those peers reporting to you eventually, and if you do, you'll want to have cultivated good relationships with them along the way.

28. Direct Reports

I know something about my direct reports and their lives outside of work.

People don't leave bad jobs, they leave bad bosses. It's easy to stick to business and focus on the tasks at hand, but that's not usually sufficient to keep people engaged. Your ability to get things done is entirely dependent on your team's level of engagement with their jobs, their commitment to the company, and their loyalty to you. Most people just need to know that someone cares about them a little, and is interested in who they are.

I have worked with very focused leaders who did not realize the way their intense focus was being interpreted by some of the people around them. If you have people on your team who have a high need for connection and acknowledgement, yet you are a task-oriented person, you're likely not providing them with the connection they need in order to perform at their best. A small investment of time and attention can be enough to fuel great performance if it's what an individual needs. In particular, any of your staff members whose job it is to interact directly with customers and/or the public likely have a high need for personal connection, so taking time with those people (salespeople, receptionists, customer care representatives) helps energize them for the important work they do representing your company.

29. Friends

I have a number of friends who've been in my life for a long time and who know they're very valuable to me even if we don't see each other often.

There's great value in having people in your life who knew you "when." Having people you can talk to without worrying about what they think is very special. If you've got them, great—take good care of them. If you had some longtime friends but you've lost contact, reach out and reengage. Class reunions are fantastic for reestablishing connections, so do your best to get to those every once in a while. Or try Facebook or LinkedIn for looking up old friends. Maintaining a connection to your roots and your history can keep you grounded and centered on your core values.

30. Board of Directors

I connect regularly with every member of my Board and work to foster positive, transparent relationships with each of them.

If you don't report directly to your company's board or advisory circle, it may not be appropriate for you to seek out your own direct relationships with members. If that's the case, give yourself full marks for this item on the assessment, but plan to revise your score when you move into a position of direct reporting and accountability to the board.

If your company does not have a formal board of directors, then perhaps there is an advisory board or similar circle of advisors. No matter who comprises that stakeholder group, this assessment item is about the relationships you have with those who provide guidance to your company.

Board members are usually chosen for their diversity of experience and background, which by definition means that you may not always see eye to eye with every individual. In spite of any differences you may have with them, your board members are valuable and worthy of your respect. Cultivating a relationship with each and every one of them will help you gain insight into what's important to them and what concerns them.

"When I took my first job as CEO almost two years ago, I made a conscious effort not to change the aspects of my life that made me successful to that point and that put me in a position to become a corporate leader. These included discipline in my work habits, diet, sleep, and exercise not to mention the relationships that were important to me personally and professionally. The transition to the CEO role is "traumatic" enough without changing

too many other aspects of one's life at the same time. The largest adjustment in assuming this role was one of isolation. As a CEO, there are no peers in the organization and I had to make concerted efforts to engage employees and Board members alike to get continual buy-in into my vision for the company and into the disciplined execution of our mission. In that regard, regularly assessing and improving the quality and structure of our team are important but I have found the impact of projecting positivity and of reinforcing core Hudbay values to employees cannot be overestimated."

—David Garafolo, President & CEO,
HudBay Minerals (hudbayminerals.com)

The Bottom Line

Good relationships don't just happen, they require effort and skill to grow and sustain. Great personal relationships can provide a valuable foundation of strength and positive energy that can sustain you through stressful times professionally. The ability to build strong personal relationships is transferable to the work world, enabling you to work with people you trust and to trust the people you work with.

4

Be a Real Leader

The higher you rise in an organization, the more people are watching you. They are watching to see what you deliver and what the company values. They're watching to see what it takes to succeed and they're watching to see what happens as a result of bad behavior. As you take on leadership roles of greater scope and scale, it's important that you think carefully about the image you're portraying and what people might be learning just from watching you.

The process of crafting your ideal leadership brand and image starts with self-awareness and the willingness to accept feedback. From there, you can make decisions about your communication and management style and the company culture you're creating. In this section, I offer what I consider to be the key elements of crafting your presence and reputation as a leader, all of which are precursors to occupying a significant leadership role. Therefore, these elements are worth crafting and fine-tuning starting early in your career.

31. Leadership Philosophy

I have a clear philosophy about leadership and I conduct myself according to that philosophy. I am an ongoing student of leadership and constantly seek examples and role models.

Your organization will respond to consistency from the top down. In order for your people to make their own determinations about how to present to you, persuade you, and work with you, they have to be able to observe consistent behavior, practices, and decisions.

Several years ago I was working with the executive team of a large health-care organization. We had done some communication style assessments using a simple model that described each person's preferred style. Most members of the team had one style they tended to prefer, and in those cases it was relatively easy for their coworkers and direct reports to know how to approach them. The CEO, however, had three styles she used regularly: a driven, big-picture style; an outgoing, gregarious style; and a caring, harmony-seeking style. Not surprisingly, it was very difficult for her team members to know how best to approach her and what tactics to use when trying to persuade her on an issue, and they could rarely predict her decisions. The recommendation? I suggested she consciously choose one style that would be her "usual" style—the one that her team members could count on when they went into meetings with her. If she was going to vary from that predominant style, it should be in exceptional situations, where her team could recognize that something extraordinary was going on.

Beneath the style is the set of beliefs that you bring to your leadership approach. Again, consistency is critical in order for your organization to know what the rules are. Your decisions can be almost predictable if your belief system and your business goals are apparent and consistent.

While having a reliable, obvious approach to leadership is important, so too is continuous learning about new ideas in leadership and incorporating useful practices into your approach. Leadership is an ongoing area of study and thought, and new ideas are always emerging. If you are serious about your continued growth and development as a leader, it is important to continue to be a student of leadership ideas and practices, whether your interest is in theoretical/academic, practical, or biographical form. That said, it's equally important not to shift your approach based on whatever book you're reading at that moment. It's tempting to adopt every exciting new idea, but that pace of change can be confusing to your team. Rather, evaluate new ideas for their relevance and appropriateness to your situation and distill your learning into evolutionary changes.

"I take full responsibility publicly for my department's activities and fully support my staff in this regard. This happens for both the good and the bad. When we receive

a 'job well done,' I always ensure that all members of the
team are recognized. I am only as good as my people!"
　　　　—Dawn Hunt, Vice President, Regulatory, Rogers
　　　　　　　　　　　　　　　　Communications, Inc.

　　　　　　　　　　　　　　　　　　　　(rogers.com)

---

32. Performance Review and 360 Degree Feedback

I have had a 360 degree feedback survey (qualitative or
quantitative) in the past two years AND have acted upon
the feedback I received. I have had a performance review
in the past year.

The more senior you are in an organization, the less likely it is
that you are offered feedback. There is a presumption that you
know what you're doing, and that you understand what you're
accountable for and will get it done. Too often there is no formal feedback process for the executive level, no review system
that evaluates the "what" and the "how." While the top leaders are there because of their experience and past successes,
the best ones are still keen to grow and learn how to be even
better, and feedback is critical to that constant improvement.

　　In order to make sure that you're continuing to grow and
improve, you need to actively seek out feedback. A 360 degree
feedback process is incredibly valuable, whether it's conducted
by third-party interview or via an anonymous questionnaire.
Asking the people who report to you and those who surround
you at the peer level and above for their thoughts about your

strengths and areas for development can provide powerful insights you can't get any other way. It's only with information that you can make the choice to change. A 360 degree feedback survey is worth doing about every two to three years, unless there has been radical change in your responsibility or in the expectations of the business.

Everybody has a boss. Whether it's a C-level executive, a board chair, an owner, or an investment consortium, most leaders have someone to whom they're accountable, in addition to their customers. That means that there's someone who can provide feedback and guidance about how to build on past performance to achieve future success. Whoever is in a position to provide you with feedback is also of an experience level to be able to offer suggestions for future improvement.

As with 360 feedback, at the most senior levels a performance review may only occur if you ask for it. And ask for it you should, at least once a year. To ensure that the process has ongoing value, take the initiative to follow the performance review with a written development plan and create an agreement to check in on it regularly.

"We are not who we think we are as leaders, we are who we are perceived to be...that is why ongoing feedback and coaching are so important to the leadership development process."

—Dale Morrison, Partner, TriPointe
Capital Partners
(tripointecapital.com)

33. Values and Walking the Talk

I live and lead by a clear set of personal values and I want to be challenged if my behavior communicates something different from those values.

When I hear frustration and dissent in an organization it is very often because of perceived "lack of integrity" at the senior leadership level. If leaders appear to be acting according to a different set of values than they expect of their employees, resentment builds quickly and loyalty evaporates. But what looks like an integrity issue can be a platform for engagement and trust if there is openness to being challenged. If you create an environment where employees at any level feel safe to question things that don't make sense or that appear inconsistent, you'll create greater engagement than ever.

Get clear on your own personal values and describe how they translate into your behavior as a leader—what fits and what doesn't. Fewer signature values are better—choose the three or four core values that you believe represent you and that you want to be known for. Communicate those values and related behaviors to your senior team, and have them cascade those messages downward throughout the organization. Engage your team in discussion about what they observe, what appears consistent, and where there's inconsistency or room for improvement. Using specific examples in your discussions will help build understanding of the type of climate you are working to create throughout the organization.

34. Core Competencies

I operate at least capably, if not masterfully, across all of the core competencies identified in our organization's leadership model. I know where my areas of development are and am taking action to improve constantly.

Most organizations have a description of the behaviors employees must demonstrate for the business to succeed—if your organization doesn't, it's something to work on! This description, called a competency model, summarizes what people in your organization need to know and do in order to be successful in your specific environment and business circumstance. In a perfect world, it is impossible to be in a position of leadership unless you are operating competently across the attributes described in your organization's model. The relative importance and emphasis of the attributes shifts and changes with role progression up the organizational hierarchy, but the desired competencies should remain consistent throughout the entire company.

When you're at or near the top, there is a reasonable expectation that you're there because you've demonstrated much, if not all, of what's defined and expected. That said, no one is perfect and you'll be more respected if you acknowledge where you need to do your development work rather than trying to pretend you've got it all figured out. Sharing your development plans, at least with your direct team, can enlist them in your process and provide a valuable role model for them to do their own work as emerging leaders.

35. "Soft" Skills

I understand that how I get things done is at least as important as what gets accomplished. I know when to coach and when to direct, when to influence and how to inspire. I listen well and know how to both give and receive feedback constructively.

I've always found it ironic that the "how" of leadership is often referred to as the "soft" skills—ironic because soft skills are usually tougher to master than technical skills. Called "behavioral competencies," soft skills are the skills required to build relationships and work effectively with other people, and include specifics like communication skills, conflict resolution, negotiation, creative problem solving, strategic thinking, team building, influencing, and persuasion. Soft skills are more transferable than technical competency, which is generally only useful within a particular functional stream. The most versatile leader is the leader who can use her people skills to lead a team to achieve results, no matter what industry or function she's in.

"I try to be really conscious of activities that help me keep a positive outlook, especially in times of stress or heavy workload. Spending time coaching members of my team, seeing them learn and achieve really 'fills up my tank,' and then I can handle stressful or difficult conversations.

Interim check-ins, measuring results or progress towards key milestones on long or complicated projects, help me keep teams on track and keep me energized. And simple things, like stepping away for a short walk or looking out the window and just disconnecting for five minutes, help me 'reset'; and then I can start again."
—Monika Federau, Senior Vice President, Marketing, Intact Insurance (intact.net)

While all soft skills are important, the willingness and ability listen well is, in my view, the most important of all. Many people progress upward in a corporate hierarchy based on masterful deployment of technical skill and knowledge shared with others. The ability to listen is not well developed because it's not used often. However, once your technical competency lands you in a position of leadership, your success will rest less on your ability to download technical information and more on your capacity to evaluate the abilities of the people around you, to support their development, and to coach them for growth, all of which start with the ability to listen well.

"I believe most leaders underestimate the value of listening—the most effective leaders understand its value and how it can differentiate them. My memories of the best managers I've had don't come from what they told

me, but rather from times when they listened to what I had to say."
—Joe Chesham, President & CEO, Northern Tower Group

From a base of good listening skills comes the ability to give and receive feedback constructively. Based on my work with leaders at all levels across a wide range of organizations, this is a vastly underdeveloped competency that results in the majority of talent development missteps and performance gaps. To be able to accept feedback graciously and deliver it with clarity and diplomacy are truly rare leadership skills that can set you apart from your peers.

36. Performance and Conduct Expectations

The people in my organization know what is expected of them and what the implications are of not meeting those expectations. We have a communication program in place to ensure expectations are clear to everyone at every level, and training/education support is available where necessary.

It's a good idea to develop and display a description of the do's and don'ts of expected behavior, whether you choose to print a detailed four-color brochure or hang a poster on the wall. Commonly referred to as a "code of conduct," these behavior guidelines should be written in plain, jargon-free language and should outline the expectations and responsibilities of every employee pertaining to coworkers, customers, the surrounding community, and other relevant stakeholders.

Once you've developed your code of conduct, you need to be sure everyone knows about and understands it. Your communication plan for your code of conduct does not have to be elaborate or complicated. What is important is that you do something to educate your teams rather than simply distribute a document and assume it's been read and understood by all. Small group discussions to ensure the intent is clear are usually sufficient, but more is better—and a process of regular review to keep it top of mind is helpful as well.

Before you go ahead and tell everyone what is expected, though, be sure all of your systems and processes are aligned with whatever you're communicating. I have seen situations where a great deal of effort went into the development and communication of a code of conduct, but the performance management system was not updated at the same time. Confusing language and inconsistent expectations between the two documents rendered the effort behind the code of conduct launch much less effective than it might have been.

37. Innovation and Creativity

I believe that relevant innovation is critical to our success. I welcome new ideas and embrace a climate in which creativity is valued and encouraged. I believe failure is an opportunity to learn.

If you're going to lead a business into the future and adapt to change when it occurs—or even anticipate it—then creating a climate in which innovation and creativity are welcome is vital.

Creativity pushes boundaries and explores uncharted territory. It takes courage to really embrace new ideas and try things that have never been done before, but the idea of possibly failing is at odds with the performance culture prevalent in most organizations these days. And you have to be comfortable with failure yourself before you can model the courage to innovate and set an example for your team.

What are your responses when a member of your team fails? Do you blame and criticize? Smile and ignore? Or do you turn it into an opportunity to learn and move forward? Have you ever failed? How did you handle it? Take a look at what really happens when something goes off the rails, because there's often a disconnect between what the company says about failure being acceptable and the actual repercussions.

Once you've created an environment where it's safe to fail, you can work on nurturing creativity. Some companies have a prearranged day or time when everyone can work on pet projects just to see what might come up. Getting out of the office as a team can be helpful, as long as you're not just swapping the bland walls of the office for the bland walls of a hotel meeting room. And finding ways to have some fun can be an easy way to get the creative juices flowing—just about everybody is more creative when they're having a good time.

"Executives today, especially those in competitive industries, need to become very good at innovation. Sustained innovation can be a great differentiator. Innovation can take different shapes: innovation in communica-

tion; innovation in management practices; innovation in recruitment and people development."

—Riaz Raihan, Senior Vice President,
Value Engineering, SAP Canada
(sap.com)

---

38. Synthesis

I can see patterns and systems in apparently disparate sets of information. I can connect the dots and lead the development of long-term, big-picture solutions.

There is a Grand Canyon–sized leap from middle to senior management in most organizations, and I have observed that the biggest change expected when people make that jump is the sudden growth of an ability to see the big picture. What we're talking about here is the ability to step back and analyze situations at a very broad, general level such that interactions between separate or seemingly unrelated elements can be observed and long-term solutions can emerge. If you are able to synthesize information and see patterns, you are able to devise a long-term strategy, a critical skill for top leaders.

The development challenge comes in helping people grow the ability to synthesize as they progress upward in their careers. People are often hired into an organization at relatively junior levels, where the job is to solve problems in a very immediate, tactical sense. Once you get really good at solving short-term problems and implementing those solutions, you get promoted and the expectations of your abilities change. Unfortunately, you rarely get the opportunity to build that skill before you're put into a role where it's required.

Developing this very necessary skill usually requires taking some initiative in order to get exposed to opportunities early on. When you're on the way up, look for projects and situations where you can start to develop the ability to synthesize— and where you can learn from others. When you're leading a team, be mindful of the need to build organizational capacity in this area and look for ways you can offer strategic opportunities to people with potential below you.

"It is about connecting the dots for sure. Amalgamating seemingly unconnected ideas into a more coherent approach and sometimes a strategy. It's about harnessing collective intelligence over individual thought."

—Matt Wickham, Vice President, National
Dealer and Ontario Consumer Sales,
Rogers Communications, Inc.
(rogers.com)

---

39. Personal Presentation and Communication Skills

I manage my appearance and work style to ensure I am setting the desired tone for others in my organization. I work continuously to hone my written and verbal communication skills to ensure I am clear and compelling at all times. I am comfortable with public speaking.

A client was recruited into a C-level role in a new company. He came from a corporate culture that was very formal in comparison with the environment he was entering. His preferred dark suits and ties, the daily uniform at his former company, did not quite fit the casual environment he was entering. His formal manner was equally at odds with his new, casually friendly workplace. While he wanted to raise the bar on expectations for his new team, in the short term his very formal approach created a barrier to building the necessary trust with his key players.

You can use your wardrobe and your mannerisms—and your office environment, your tone in e-mail, and your meeting behaviors—as tools to communicate and send messages. The surface attributes of appearance and behavior can send messages about what you expect. They can also be a way to build relationships and break down barriers. You can choose a personal style as a way to be similar or as a way to be different. You can require formal meeting behavior or let things be casual, expect neat workspaces or allow the "creatively haphazard." Most importantly, you need to understand that everyone around you will be observing and evaluating the way you present yourself and the kind of environment you create, and they will be drawing conclusions from every bit of it.

Equally important, both inside and outside your organization, is your ability to deliver a message with clarity and conviction. Presentation skills and public speaking abilities only increase in importance as you rise in responsibility. Take a course, rehearse for every major occasion, and get feedback. Practice really does make a difference.

40. Personal Story

I know how to tell my personal success story in a way that aligns with my leadership brand and reflects my personal values.

Every leadership brand has to be built on a foundation. Your personal story of success can be that foundation. Because you have risen to the level of senior executive and are an ambassador for careers within your organization, many people both inside and outside your company will be curious to know about your climb up the ladder. You may also be asked to teach or speak on the basis of that story. It's therefore incredibly important and useful to think about your story before you are asked to tell it, so that you're prepared and can touch on the important points. Reflect on your story occasionally and ensure that it achieves its intended goals. Also, be sure you tell it similarly every time you're asked, because discrepancies and omissions will confuse your audience and get in the way of establishing a clear leadership brand.

"If you are a leader who wants to motivate people to take action, then you must do more than excite their

*minds—you need to speak to their hearts too. This is
exactly what a good story does."*

—Jacqueline Foley, Stories That Stick
(jacquelinefoley.com)

The Bottom Line

Good leaders demonstrate clarity, consistency, and focus,
starting with their own beliefs and behaviors. Consider all
the touch points and opportunities for impact that you have,
and realize how important it is that you craft every message
you're sending so it creates the impression you intend. Resist
the temptation to dive down into the weeds, revert to habitual
behavior, and let your game face slip. While it's all right to be
human, it's not all right to let an impulse or a poorly chosen set
of words tear down your credibility.

5

Put the Business Basics in Place

If you enjoyed traditional business education and formal blue chip corporate training, what follows here will seem obvious. Be that as it may, basic business disciplines and operational practices are table stakes, and are worth calling out in specific relief as we talk about how to be successful in a holistic, well-rounded way. And if you're not at the top yet, there is no time like the present to start operating from a strong set of basic tools and processes.

41. Vision

My organization or team has a clear vision for the long-term impact we are striving to make, and every employee knows and understands the vision.

In his 2010 book, *Drive*, Dan Pink summarizes the three things most people need from their work as "autonomy, mastery, and purpose." They need to be able to make decisions, use their best skills, and know that they're part of something bigger than themselves. That bigger thing is most often described in a company vision statement. A "vision" is a desired future state of the world—it doesn't yet exist. It's big—bigger than any one person or company—and so cannot possibly be achieved by anyone working independently. A vision represents a huge stretch, but it's a scenario that's possible—if it were achieved it would mean that a major problem had been solved or an issue resolved. So if your company has a clear vision of some utopian future state of the world, it's easy for your employees to get on board with it; or, conversely, to know for sure that it's not what they are able to support and opt out. An example is the vision attributed to Bill Gates when he was running Microsoft. "A computer on every desk and in every home" describes a world that does not yet exist, but which is possible; and while it's not something Microsoft can achieve on its own, the company's efforts can contribute to that vision becoming reality one day in the future.

Too often I've seen inwardly focused goal statements being touted as "vision." I personally worked for three different organizations that claimed being "the best food company" as their vision. Ill-defined, nonspecific, and self-serving, that sort of vision statement is not something employees can get excited about. On the other hand, Ikea's "Affordable solutions for better living" and Walt Disney's original vision of a place where "parents and children can have fun together" are examples of aspirational future states that are easy to imagine and equally easy for every employee to adopt and work toward.

Unfortunately, according to an article by Teresa Amabile and Steven Kramer in the January 2012 issue of *McKinsey Quarterly*, senior executives often interfere with their employees' engagement in meaningful work. By defaulting to mediocre tactics, micromanaging, changing strategy frequently, lacking coordination, and setting misbegotten, irrelevant goals, an organization's leaders can get in the way of employees getting engaged around a meaningful vision.

The key is to establish a vision that employees at every level in the organization can relate to and get excited about. Once you've established it, though, the next—and even more important—step is ensuring that every employee knows and understands it. Too often, the communication of vision stops partway down the hierarchy, possibly on the assumption that lower-level employees won't understand or care. In fact, your organization's performance is more consistent and more sustainable if every employee at every level is walking the talk with conviction.

The stories of Four Seasons Hotels' commitment to vision are legendary, as are those of Southwest Airlines. But great stories of front-line employees putting the vision into action are everywhere. Take the example of Zingerman's Roadhouse, a small restaurant chain in Michigan, described in *Harvard Business Review* by Gretchen Spreitzer and Christine Porath. When challenged as to whether the average waiter could reasonably be expected to know or understand strategy, one of Zingerman's cofounders asked a nearby busboy to share the company's vision. Sure enough, the teenager was able to describe it in his own words, and he even knew how well the kitchen was performing that week against some of their key measures. There's a good chance that busboy also knew how his job could affect that performance—powerful stuff.

42. Mission

My organization or team knows what we're good at and how we will work to advance our vision. Each employee understands how he can contribute.

Once you have articulated the vision, your organization needs to get clear on exactly what its role will be in achieving that vision. To extend the Microsoft example, Microsoft builds software that makes computers work well and helps us live our lives and do our work better. Microsoft is not building the boxes or selling computers in stores. The company knows what it does and it focuses on doing that core thing extremely well. Do you know what your organization does incredibly well, and are you focused on doing that and only that? Or do you try to do whatever it is that strikes you as a brilliant idea, independent of whether your organization is really good at it?

Every organization has some key things that it knows how to do really well, ideally better and differently than any close competitors. You and your team will be most successful if you focus on doing that thing you do best—and if your focus can be distilled into a single statement, there's a pretty good chance you're onto something. The ideal mission statement is very simple and describes your company at its essence, the thing that you do better than anyone else, the thing you want to be best known for. It should identify your primary target, specify the service or product you provide to that target, and describe what is unique about your offering or combination of offerings. Your mission statement helps both customers and employees understand what business you're in, and creates a set of criteria for decision making. Some examples of well-constructed mission statements are:

- Apple is committed to bringing the best personal computing experience to students, educators, creative professionals, and consumers around the world through its innovative hardware, software, and Internet offerings.
- Dell's mission is to be the most successful computer company in the world at delivering the best customer experience in markets we serve.
- Facebook's mission is to give people the power to share and make the world more open and connected.
- Google's mission is to organize the world's information and make it universally accessible and useful.

It's critical that every employee or team member be able to contextualize her own role and contribution in terms of the company mission.

43. Strategic Plan

My organization or team has a strategic plan and we review it annually.

The strategic plan is the map, the set of directions that helps the organization orient itself, prioritize, and make resource decisions. Strategy is typically set for the medium to long term, however, in order to ensure its ongoing relevance, you and your direct team must review it annually and revise if necessary. And, remember, a plan is just that—it's not fixed. But if a plan is created well, it's founded on sufficient data to ensure that it is relevant. The strategic plan reflects the vision, mission, and company values and outlines the plan to achieve a long-term business goal based on those core elements.

Your strategic planning process will be strongest if it starts with a process of analyzing the business. A basic SWOT (strengths, weaknesses, opportunities, and threats) analysis can provide at least a preliminary foundation for the strategy discussion. From there, you can envision the goals for the future, describe the size of the gap between where you are now and where you want to be, and define actions intended to get you to that desired outcome over a specific period of time.

44. Five-Year Targets and Goals

We have metrics in place to measure our growth and success five years into the future, and we examine those metrics annually and revise as appropriate. We do not react to short-term aberrations in the marketplace—we evaluate their impact on our long-term plan and course correct only if necessary.

Long-term success measures, tied to strategy, can ensure the business is on track in spite of short-term aberrations. Airline pilots, while apparently flying a straight course from takeoff to landing, are constantly course correcting when they're in the sky to compensate for the short-term effects of wind and weather. Similarly, you may find a need to make occasional adjustments to your plans in order to stay on track toward your long-term goals, however make changes only after carefully evaluating marketplace activity. If you react to every hiccup in the market you'll use your company resources inefficiently, not to mention confuse your teams with constant changes in direction.

45. One-Year Operating Plan

My organization or team has a one-year operating plan and we have the resources in place to execute against that plan.

The logical step following a strategic plan is an operating plan, which gets specific about the nuts and bolts required to deliver that year's portion of the strategic plan. The operating plan identifies—and is often the basis of a request for—the budget and resources required to deliver on the year's objectives. A good operating plan describes the activities that will be undertaken and the breakdown of funds required for each of those activities. It provides a link between the more conceptual and higher-level strategic plan and the nuts and bolts of what the business or operating unit actually does on a day-to-day or week-to-week basis throughout the year. The operating plan describes resource allocation and new resource requirements. It reflects recent marketplace or environmental changes that have an impact on the achievability of the strategic plan. Operating plans can—and should—be crafted at the "doing" level of the organization, not at the executive level, with significant dialogue between departments and business units to ensure alignment. Oversight and sponsorship by the executive level ensures integration of departmental plans up into the broader organizational plan. A fulsome operating plan includes the one-year objectives, the activities intended to achieve the objectives, the due dates for the activities, staffing requirements, and measures of success.

46. Talent Review and Succession Plan

My organization or team has annual talent reviews and has successors identified—and prepared—for all key positions, including my own. We value, and seek, diversity across our entire workforce.

A talent review is the core of your talent management strategy. It is a regular—ideally annual—look at who you've got, what they're good at, where they need to develop, and where you've got gaps, all in the context of the business strategy and operating plan. Talent reviews are crucially important for ensuring the sustainability and long-term viability of your organization; however, they often are postponed or rushed because they are not directly related to the day-to-day functioning of the business. My coaching work with organizations in recent years has focused on accelerating the development of less experienced, high-potential individuals to prepare them to move into senior leadership roles more quickly than they might if left to develop at their own pace. The fact is, with talent reviews and development planning falling in priority in favor of more urgent business needs, it's no surprise that it's difficult to find a "ready now" leader to assign if an opening suddenly arises.

One of the hallmarks of a good leader is her ability to hire and develop talent in such a way that the promise of the fresh talent pool equals or exceeds the leader's own capabilities. Being known as a leader who can nurture the potential in people and ultimately build organizational capacity is to be known as a leader who creates long-term value.

"Hire Gretzkys.* Surround yourself with people who are better than you are. They will challenge the status quo, push you harder, and ensure that you are looking around the right corners. Importantly, they will help you drive accelerated performance today. Even better, they will provide you with more gratification than you could ever imagine as you watch their professional development. It really is the most rewarding aspect of any leader's job. Just be prepared for them to ask for your job."

—Tom Greco, President, Frito-Lay North America

---

* Referring to the great hockey player Wayne Gretzky

Truly progressive talent-planning strategies include an understanding of how diversity must be addressed, and are clear that a diverse workforce is a business and competitive advantage. The best teams have complementary skill sets, backgrounds, and perspectives, and leaders of high-performing organizations understand and hire for that complementarity, without fear of or discomfort with the unfamiliar or dissimilar.

47. Measures of Success

My organization or team knows, and measures, the factors beyond the financial goals that will ensure we stay on track toward our objectives.

Employee engagement, customer satisfaction, share price—all are metrics beyond revenue and market share that can be indicators of business success, and all are relevant measures of aspects of the business that impact overall success.

One relatively new metric that is starting to show up at the global economic level is gross national happiness—a measure for a country's ability to sustain success and enjoy progress and positive development. With the growing body of research on the impact of happiness on employee performance and satisfaction, perhaps employee engagement scores will start becoming a lead indicator of whether a company has the potential to be successful.

48. Crisis Management Plan

My organization or team has a formal plan in place to deal with emergencies and unforeseen events, both internal and external to the company.

A crisis management plan is the corporate equivalent of insurance and a will. Reputations are made and lost based on response to crisis. Think of the difference between Tylenol, whose brand recovered from a product tampering incident, and British Petroleum subsequent to the oil spill in the Gulf of Mexico. Your organization should have written plans in place and key players informed as to their role should an issue arise.

"A written crisis management plan provides the organizing principle around how a company should manage a crisis. Theory in such plans is useless. It needs to contain values, roles, tasks, and messages that will help companies move faster to decision making and proactive management at the time of a crisis."

—Linda Smith, President and CEO, SmithCom
Communications (www.smithcom.ca)

49. Corporate Social Responsibility Plan

My organization or team has a clear point of view on issues that we support and we have programs in place to support those causes.

It's no longer enough for a company to provide good products and services. Nowadays, consumers make decisions based on their perception of the integrity of the companies they buy from. Corporate social responsibility (CSR) is not about having a well-publicized charitable giving program or encouraging your employees to volunteer, although both of those activities are worthwhile. Corporate social responsibility starts with the basics of how your organization conducts its normal business. According to CSR blogger and consultant Mallen Baker (mallenbaker .net), CSR is about how companies manage their business processes to produce an overall positive impact on society.

50. Technology Plan

My organization has a plan to ensure we stay current and effective in our use of technology to support our business, both internally and externally. We understand how to apply technology to support productivity, process and systems management, customer connections, and employee recruitment/retention.

A technology plan, like a talent management plan, should be one component of your long-term strategic plan, with the specifics called out for the coming year in the operating plan. With the rapid change in available tools for communication and productivity, it's tempting for organizations (or, more likely, individual teams or departments within organizations) to become fascinated with the latest gadget and attempt to introduce it without planning or preparation. And there's almost always someone in an organization who thinks he knows better than the IT department, or at least can get things done faster than IT.

The fact is, technology—well planned and well deployed— can provide incredible tools for supporting productivity, for connecting with customers, for recruitment, for almost every aspect of business. A technology plan establishes a clearly defined position on what role technology plays in the strategic plan and how it will be resourced. I call this item out separately because, although it must be embedded in the strategic and operating plans, technology is often assumed, implied, ignored, or overindulged.

The Bottom Line

The items in this chapter represent some of the strategy and process elements that are foundational for a well-run team or organization, and that, as a leader, are your responsibility to create or ensure are in place. Most large organizations will have all of them in position already. If you are on your way up, however, it's never too late to start implementing many of these processes on a small scale within the team for which you have responsibility. If that's the case, be mindful of the overall corporate strategy and plans, and ensure that whatever you develop for your area of responsibility is a logical cascade from the plans that have been developed at the very top. Full alignment with organizational strategy and flawless planning for and execution of business imperatives are what it takes to move up.

6

Take Charge of Your Career

A great career, aligned with your personal goals and offering fulfillment on every level, doesn't just happen. It
requires thought and planning, evaluation and revision, context and perspective. It also requires openness to opportunity,
a willingness to make strategic moves, and an understanding
of when it's appropriate to take risks in service of a longer-
term goal. Self-awareness is critical, as is openness to feedback
and the ability to learn from others and from adversity.

Sometimes, your best moves are the ones you didn't see
coming—with a good sense of general direction and confidence
in your inner compass and gut instincts, the unexpected can bear
brilliant results. The happiest and most successful executives I
know admit to having had a plan *and* a willingness to abandon it
or go in an entirely surprising direction when it seemed the right
thing to do. If you address all of the items in this section, you'll
be well positioned to choose a career path that fulfills you and
enables you to satisfy your professional and personal goals.

51. Career Plan

I am clear about what I need to accomplish in order to feel that I have been successful in my career, and I have short- and medium-term goals that are part of that plan. I have set approximate timing milestones for each goal.

Having a career plan means that you have a general template against which to make decisions and take actions. That said, a plan that is too rigid may cause you to miss opportunities for learning and experiences that weren't on your radar but that might have tremendous value. So the idea is to have a directional plan—a career road map—that has a clear end goal and milestone markers along the way, but that can be achieved via several different routes.

52. Personal/Professional Goal Alignment

My career plan aligns with and contributes to my overall personal life plan.

A career plan is *not* a life plan. Career is one piece of the puzzle—an important piece, to be sure, but one piece. A big career decision can be easy to make if it aligns well with your life plan, or it can provoke stress if it's not clear how it fits in the bigger picture.

Presuming you've created some sort of vision for your life (see chapter 2), it's worthwhile to check in every so often on the fit between that plan and your career. And it's even better if that check-in is, at least in part, a conversation with your spouse or other significant person in your life. You'll probably find that the people who care about you can see things about what you're doing and how you're behaving that aren't obvious to you.

53. Passion for the Business

I believe in my organization's mission and vision and I am passionate about the business we're in. I am my company's best salesperson.

I met with the CEO of a client company to get his feedback on one of the executives I was coaching. The first thing he asked was whether I was a customer of their service. When my response was negative, he asked why—and I responded that, until that moment, no one had asked. Given that I was working with several senior-level people in the company at the time, the CEO found this a bit perplexing. He asked my permission to divert his attention for a moment, whereupon he sent several quick e-mails to his people "inquiring" about this situation. Sure enough, my customer needs were addressed at my next coaching session, and the CEO's modeling of advocacy and passion for the business at every available opportunity did not go unnoticed in the senior ranks.

"Absolute identity with one's cause is the first and great condition of successful leadership."

—Woodrow Wilson

As a top-level executive, you are the most public representative of your company's product or service. If you don't love it and believe in it enough to get the whole world on board, you may not be in the right place.

And even if you do love your business, there still might be something else required to make you feel like you're doing what you're meant to do. A career sales executive worked for Fortune 500 companies and then owned a mid-sized company with two business partners. He was always very successful and believed in the products he represented, however he wouldn't have described himself as having real passion for his work. After selling his business, he found himself at a crossroads when an unusual opportunity arose. This opportunity was a good fit with his skills, would require a moderate but reasonable stretch because it had greater scope and scale than he'd tackled previously, and was in a line of business he felt he understood. All that said, it was unconventional, offered only average compensation, and would require taking some risk. When analyzed logically, the decision wasn't clear. But there was something about the idea of this new role that excited him—something that caused him to feel like this unique opportunity was what he was "meant" to do. Six months later he would describe his new role as "the best thing I've ever done" and say, "I'm working harder than I ever have, yet it feels so easy."

The best career decisions are made with a combination of head and heart (or gut, or whatever body part it is that speaks to you). The job that seems most logically appropriate, if not accompanied by a visceral level of excitement, will probably not be a job you'll love. And if you don't get up in the morning feeling excited about going to work, you're probably not doing the right work in the right place, and it will be tough to lead others credibly.

54. Resumé

I have an up-to-date resumé.

A resumé's usefulness is not limited to job hunting. It's a marketing document, whether you're testing the job waters, applying for a board role, or simply ensuring that your current company's files are up to date. Even if you're an entrepreneur and not worried about marketing yourself into a job, many banks and venture capital companies require resumés from business leaders seeking funding.

A strong resumé leads with a summary paragraph that describes who you are as a business leader. Following the summary is a list of your key accomplishments, using active language and metrics where available (and where not bound by confidentiality). Even if you're in the same job year after year, you should update your accomplishments annually so the document is always current.

Of course, a resumé is critical when you are looking to change jobs, but don't leave preparing it until that time. According to Martin Buckland of Elite Resumés (aneliteresume.com), you are in the best frame of mind to prepare a resumé when you are gainfully employed and successful. Your head is clearer, you are able to focus on your successes and talk about them positively, and you've got your accomplishments top of mind. Buckland also recommends keeping a "brag book" at home that you update regularly. This ensures you've got a record of where and when you've had impact, so you don't have to scramble if you should suddenly need that information. And it's best to be prepared—no matter how successful you are, the business world is unpredictable and every executive is disposable. Don't be caught off guard.

55. Salary and Market Value

I am comfortable with my compensation and know where I stand in the external marketplace based on my role, organization, industry, and location.

Compensation is based on scope, scale, geography, complexity, risk, tenure, experience, and many other factors. If you have changed jobs in the past five years or so you've probably got an accurate gauge of whether your compensation is competitive. However, if you've climbed the ladder inside one organization for many years, you might be surprised to learn what it would cost your organization to replace you with an external candidate. Don't underestimate your value.

It's important that money is a nonissue—your feelings about what you're being paid should never dominate your feelings about whether or not you enjoy your work. Your compensation needs to be fair and relevant in the marketplace. Money can be a very emotional issue and if you are at all resentful about how you think you're being treated, that resentment will tend to color the way you think about other challenges in your role.

If you haven't checked how your compensation measures up in the marketplace, an executive recruiter can often give you a general sense of what someone in your role is worth. There are also useful websites, such as Salary.com and Monster.com, that make salary data available.

56. Recruiter Connections

I know who the major recruiters are in my area, by both functional and sector specialty, and I have connections to all of them.

Recruiters are successful—or not—based on their connections and insights into who's who in organizations. They are fantastic sources of insight and can be great links to opportunities. Their currency is information, so if you can be helpful when they call, you'll be on their list to contact when the plum opportunities cross their desks. They can also help you find talent and build your own team, and they'll be better equipped to do that if they understand what kind of leader you are and what sort of culture you've created in your organization.

If you don't already have recruiter connections, it's worthwhile to try to establish a few key ones. Most major firms maintain online databases and have the capability to upload resumés from their websites, making it easy to get yourself on file with the major players in your field. When you receive a call, make it clear that you're not actively looking but that you do want to establish some relationships. The experienced search people know that just making and maintaining connections is valuable.

57. Lessons from Adversity

I have reflected on the challenges I've encountered along my professional journey and I understand the learning opportunity embedded in each of those challenges.

If you've been working for any length of time, it's almost guaranteed that you've had a few difficult, if not humiliating, experiences—and if not at work, then in life. What you do with those experiences is more important than whether or not they happened. Your ability to interpret your negative experiences as learning moments will enable you to share them with others as teachable stories.

I attended an executive development off-site event with the senior team of a client company, at which their CEO conducted a "fireside chat." He spent an hour telling stories from his career and life, sharing his path to the top with the key people in his organization. The aspect of his talk that had the greatest impact was his absolute transparency about the challenges he had faced along the way. He truly felt that his most difficult experiences had been fundamental to his development as a leader, and he believed that his executive team would gain valuable insight by learning about some of the adversity he'd faced and how he'd handled it. He was right—feedback from the attendees after the event cited the CEO's stories as the most powerful and impactful element of the program.

58. "Elevator Speech"

I have a summary statement about who I am professionally and can distinguish that from what I do.

Ever meet someone at a conference or a party and regret asking, "So what do you do?" You should always be prepared to take advantage of an opportunity to connect with interesting new contacts—and they'll be interested in maintaining the connection if you don't bore them silly at the first meeting. And, even more importantly, if you find yourself serendipitously confronted with someone you really want to impress or with whom you'd like a strong professional connection, having a summary statement at the ready may prove useful.

A client had targeted a particular company as part of her job search. In preparation for approaching the firm, she dropped by their office to get a look at their environment and see if she could pick up some printed information. While she was chatting with the receptionist, the president of the company walked by. The receptionist introduced the job searcher, who then had the opportunity to ride down in, yes, the elevator with the president. Without a good summary statement she would have had to chat about the weather—instead, she made a connection, got permission to send her resumé directly to him, and ultimately ended up working for the company.

59. Skills Inventory

I know what I'm good at and am able to comfortably discuss my strengths.

There's a fine line between confidence and arrogance. Arrogance is having lots of flash but little substance. Confidence indicates that you're clear about the value you offer and the positive impact you can have on an organization. Reflect on your accomplishments, both career and personal. What did it take for you to achieve the various things you've done in your life? Bear in mind that skills used outside of work can have relevance to your career. The planning and discipline required to train for and participate in an adventure race, for example, can translate into dedication to completing a difficult project at work. Supervising the renovation of a house provides evidence of excellent budgeting, project management, and team leadership skills. Take the time to list the things you do well, in their most transferable language. Prepare examples of your strongest skills and competencies in action, with metrics wherever possible.

The higher up you go in leadership, the more your skills are defined by the "how" you get things done, rather than technical, functional, or subject matter-based expertise. In your reflections in the exercise above, think about what made your approach to using those skills different from the approach someone else would have taken. Your goal here is to define your uniqueness wherever possible, and to paint an aspirational picture for the next level of your team.

60. Role Models

I know which companies and/or leaders I respect and who I'd like to learn from in the future.

No matter where you are in your career, there are always people and organizations you can look to as examples of what you value. Knowing who you respect and which companies are generating great results can give you examples to use as inspiration in your current role and organization. And your choice of role models and examples of leadership excellence can be instructive to people in your organization—it will help them understand what you're trying to create. The earlier you develop your list of people you admire, the greater the chance you can connect with them at some point over the course of your career.

The Bottom Line

Never assume your career is going to take care of itself. If you are well prepared to meet whatever opportunities arise, and if you make your decisions based on a well-thought-out strategy, leaving yourself open to unexpected and exciting possibilities, you'll set yourself up to achieve the things that are really important to you.

7

Build a Valuable Network

Having a network is different from networking. Networking has a bad reputation, and that's primarily because most people don't do it well. No executive at a high level does anything called networking. So it's vital to set aside the idea of networking as an activity and start focusing on building the critical business asset that is your network. Building a strong and valuable network requires constant effort and attention and is an ongoing process—it's never done. "Networking" is a vague, often pointless activity; "building your network" is more concrete. Start early and consider the time invested in building your network as having lifelong value.

The people in your network will come from every part of your life—every colleague you've ever worked with, every friend you've ever made, and every neighbor you've ever had. It will grow through connections with the people you know through your kids, your parents, your siblings, and your other family members. You just never know when a connection in your network will lead you to another, helpful one, creating potential future business value.

Most people view their network as a resource—and indeed it is—but before it can become that you must build it and contribute to the people in it, starting as early as possible in your career. Contributing to your network is what makes it strong. If you only ever take from your network, it will be too weak to support you when you need it. I've experienced this many times with people in my own network, and I've stepped away from some professional relationships where the other person was only interested in what she could get. Others will see through a self-centered attitude just as quickly.

Instead, think about what you have to contribute and the benefits you offer to someone who connects with you. A strong network is about give and take. This chapter serves as a list of the top ten elements that will help you create a strong, sustainable, valuable network—one that you can benefit from and be generous with. For an excellent additional resource on developing valuable business relationships, check out *Relationship Economics* by David Nour.

61. Tools

I've got an active, up-to-date LinkedIn profile. I understand and have evaluated Twitter's usefulness to my network-building efforts. I am aware of and use the other connection tools common in my professional arena.

With more than 135 million members in over two hundred countries around the world, LinkedIn is one of the most powerful business tools in existence. This social media platform makes it very easy to find people who have the knowledge or experience you may want to access. And it's free! While some people in my network do make use of the premium features, the basic account fulfills my purposes of visibility in a certain population and access to resources when I need them.

Whenever I'm working with a client who is thinking about changing jobs, the first thing we look at is her LinkedIn profile. We'll update her photo, rework her summary paragraph, and get her on a regular schedule of making new connections. It's much easier to stay current if you keep up with these tasks on an ongoing basis.

When crafting your LinkedIn profile, consider the image you are creating and the types of messages you want your network to receive. Your LinkedIn profile represents more than just your bio and photo; it's everything visitors see when they visit your page, including activity such as your new connections and status updates, and also the many add-ons you can choose to display, such as your travel destinations, the books you're reading, or your latest blog post. Just remember that LinkedIn is a professional network, so be sure that anything you're posting is relevant to and appropriate for a business audience.

Be sure your work experience and summary paragraph are up to date and reflect the most current version of who you are as a businessperson and what's unique and valuable about what you do. If you're interested in a certain kind of role make sure to include the keywords people would search with when they want to find candidates for such a position. Test out those search terms yourself by typing them into LinkedIn and seeing who comes up. If those seem like your peers, you've found the right words. Now make yourself stand out!

LinkedIn is intended to be a two-way street, so make it clear what you're interested in, whether it's reconnecting with former colleagues, learning about new business opportunities, or making specific kinds of connections. In return, make it easy for people to identify you as the kind of resource you are willing and able to be, so you can make the types of contributions that are important to you. I often get questions about executive coaching, and I'm happy to be a resource in that setting.

Put a schedule in place to ensure that your LinkedIn profile changes regularly. This doesn't need to take longer than ten minutes, and you can do it as little as once a week or as often as daily. Find a schedule that works for you.

Twitter is used by many to reach out into business communities and ask for information and resources. If key players in your industry use it, be sure you're there too—you may be missing connections and business opportunities if you're not in the same communication stream. The same logic applies if there are Internet forums or communication tools particular to your field or industry. Be sure you're aware of and taking advantage of the tools that will drive the most value for time spent.

62. Alumni Association

I belong to the alumni association from my alma mater and keep my contact information up to date with them.

Most people who attended business school understand that it's useful to stay in touch, because you never know where your former classmates will end up and how your careers may intersect in mutually beneficial ways. But consider for a moment the rest of the world—elementary school, high school, college, professional schools, technical and specialized programs. Most learning environments have some sort of alumni connection program to make it easy to stay in touch with former classmates.

It's useful to stay connected with the school, as well as with your classmates. Often, when you reach a certain level of visibility and success, your alma mater will want to highlight you as a resource or invite you to speak or to teach a class. This is a great opportunity to give back and also to gain more visibility by speaking at a homecoming or commencement event. You're reinforcing your value and also demonstrating to students what's possible. All schools are very proud of their successful alumni, as thriving graduates attest to the value of the school, and they are happy to help you build your reputation this way.

"There is genuine value in staying actively engaged with your alma mater—it provides a vibrant community for

networking, conducting business, and access to innovative research."

—Terri Garton, Director of Alumni Relations,
Richard Ivey School of Business
(ivey.uwo.ca)

---

63. Professional Groups

I am an active member of my professional association.

Professional groups provide an opportunity to keep your skills sharp and to pursue ongoing development and improvement. They help you to stay current on the best practices in your industry and connected to what's going on there. Their programs sometimes offer the continuing education credits you need to maintain your professional designation and credentials. Annual conferences can be an occasion to reconnect with people you already know as well as to meet newer entrants to your field, and can be excellent recruitment opportunities if your organization is on the lookout for new talent.

Industry events and publications also keep you connected with like-minded people in fields you were/are interested in, so you can hear about leading and cutting-edge practices. As another dimension of your network, professional groups give you the opportunity to meet people who will be a resource for others in your network, and that makes you more valuable.

In many cases, the people you're meeting at professional events are competitors, but they are useful connections. Having access to resources to make referrals is always helpful, as is the opportunity to have conversations about industry and technical trends. Or, at minimum, follow the advice of Sun Tzu, the ancient Chinese military leader: "Keep your friends close and your enemies closer."

64. Lunches/Casual Meetings

I have a schedule of regular breakfast/lunch/coffee meetings that keep me connected with people outside my immediate circle of peers, friends, and colleagues.

Casual meetings are where relationships really get built, though I do suggest caution about saying yes to too many invitations that just don't make sense. Even though I may have empathy for the difficulties of new entrepreneurs, and am flattered to be asked to share my experience, I simply cannot accept every request to meet informally to discuss someone's new business or client challenge.

When you're in a high-demand role in an organization, it's easy to get really inwardly focused. You go to the same place every day, do what's required, and don't get out at all. You'll stick your head into the office next door for a quick chat or to offer a lunch invitation, but never walk down the hall or to another floor to interact with someone new. Relationships are not built by e-mail: step outside your immediate circle of peers, friends, and colleagues.

When it comes to the relationships you truly value and want to develop, make a point of getting out in the world to spend time with those people. Some executives schedule two a week, while others make their meetings less frequent but still regular. Just get these dates into your schedule and get out there. Make a list of the people you really enjoy spending time with, those you learn a lot from and who learn a lot from you. Stretch yourself to get that important outside perspective. And don't forget to have a good time! For further thinking on this idea, check out Keith Ferrazzi's *Never Eat Alone.*

65. Introductions and Recommendations

I have clear criteria to apply when I receive requests to use my network to assist others.

The stronger your network, the more people will want to tap into it. This is particularly relevant for LinkedIn, but also to other requests you will get. You have to think very carefully about who you'll help and why. Your reputation is highly connected to how you use introductions, and you don't want to risk damaging it. Think twice about introducing people you don't know, unless they've been highly recommended by someone you know and respect.

Have a set of rules or criteria that help you know what to do when someone asks for access to a contact in your network. That way you won't have to think it through every time.

Your network is an asset. You always want to build it up, not tear it down, and making a bad recommendation or introduction is risky. If things don't work out, it can really damage your relationship with that contact. When you make a good recommendation, on the other hand, you enhance your reputation and help reinforce your network value to others.

66. Responsiveness to Requests

I have clear criteria regarding how and to whom I will respond when I receive requests for my time or connections.

When people make a request, there's a reason for it—at least in their minds. Journalists, for example, typically need answers right away, and it's useful to be known as a valuable resource to the media. Job hunters, on the other hand, are often casting a very wide net, and may or may not be useful connections or appropriate expenditures of your time or network capital. Have criteria in place and know who's in the inner circle of people who get your quickest response time. You don't have to be on top of everything for everybody, but a courteous note to acknowledge the request is always a nice touch, whether or not you feel you are able to assist the person.

67. Requests for Information or Resources

I reach out into my network if I need information or a connection.

Your network is an asset, and you can receive from it as well. So if you need something, you shouldn't hesitant to reach out to your network and ask. It sounds simple, but people don't do it. If you need a resource or a referral, rather than going through directory listings or doing a web search, put it out to your network, "Does anyone know a good...in the area?" If you've contributed regularly as a resource for others, there's no reason not to ask for help.

Some people only use their network for their own gain, but the flip side is just as questionable. Why bother maintaining your network and investing that time unless you're claiming a return on that investment? People like to help—it's human nature—so let them!

68. Maintenance

I have a process for connecting into my network on a regular basis.

My network on LinkedIn sees something new from me at least a couple of times a week. Whether I've added someone new to my network, posted an update, or talked about the latest leadership book I'm reading, I'm staying visible and active.

Maybe you're someone who likes going to parties, or perhaps you build great relationships over quieter one-on-one lunches. Or maybe you're extraordinarily charismatic on the phone—whatever works well for you, use it to your advantage. One coach I know makes ten phone calls every Monday morning, without fail. He usually leaves a voice-mail message, just saying hello, but occasionally he'll catch someone live and have a quick catch-up chat. No matter what method you prefer, keep connecting on a regular basis. This is about watering your network "garden."

69. Club Memberships

I know which local clubs are the best for meeting useful contacts with common interests.

I see it at five a.m. every day at the gym. Several investment bankers line up on the exercise cycles, the onboard television sets tuned to the global money market report. Another group of individuals, all senior sales executives of varying backgrounds, convene on the elliptical machines. The health-care group can be found on the treadmills. The conversations are largely business-based, but with some boundaries—many of these people are direct competitors. They are sharing market insights and people news ("gossip," in some circles) and debating upcoming elections based on the anticipated impact on their respective businesses. These are conversations they wouldn't have with coworkers over the course of a typical day, and they're having them with people they would not have met had they not joined this particular executive fitness facility. And I'm sure you can guess why I'm there!

Check for fitness clubs near your home and your office, as well as for specialized clubs in areas relevant to your own interests—golf courses, sailing clubs, ski clubs, curling clubs. There are lots of choices. If you can combine the pursuit of something you enjoy with an opportunity to meet interesting and potentially useful people, you'll be reaping the best of all worlds. But don't join a club just to meet its members—you'll be easy to spot if you have an agenda other than the hobby that is a passion to the others, and you'll quickly lose credibility.

70. Network Management

I know which companies and individuals, with which skill sets and knowledge bases, I want in my network, and I have a plan to expand it to include them. I examine my network regularly and have a process for weeding out people who are no longer relevant or desirable.

Based on your business plan and professional goals, what kind of additions to your network do you need? Planning the expansion of your network is a much more strategic and intentional approach to building your network than most people ever undertake. The fact is that your network is most valuable when it is being used both to support your current business and your future professional goals. For the purposes of your company's best interests, think in terms of future strategic initiatives and potential future resources or partnerships. Go looking for connections within your network for those people who will be useful in the future. A similar approach can be taken when it comes to supporting your own career progression. If there's a company you'd like to lead or an industry you'd like to move toward, start now to build relationships in those key areas.

If maintenance is about watering your network garden, then culling is about weeding that garden. Every once in a while you'll find there are people who are asking too much or asking inappropriately. Just as it's okay to divorce friends who no longer fit into your life, you can weed out people from your professional network. Start by just cooling down your correspondence with the person, by not replying to messages. That may solve the issue. In some cases, you'll want or need to actually disconnect. You can explain, "I appreciate that you have a need, however I feel that I've supported you as much as I have the capacity for."

The point is to make sure every person in your network has a reason to be there, just as you always want to be earning a place in other people's networks.

The Bottom Line

Your network, like any other asset, requires attention and maintenance to grow in value. Take good care of it, manage it strategically, and be generous with its resources and it will serve you well throughout your entire career.

8

Be a Lifelong Learner

I've never met a leader with a big vision who didn't also have a huge commitment to his own development. Anyone who's trying to stay at the top of his game never stops learning—he never presumes he knows it all, and he's not embarrassed to seek wisdom from others. In fact, outstanding leaders know that the best way to stay sharp is to be constantly in pursuit of learning and new ideas.

This concept of always staying in a learning mind-set was best highlighted by Stephen Covey in *The Seven Habits of Highly Effective People*, which put forth the idea of "sharpening the saw." Focusing on your own growth will ensure you've got an ever-expanding set of tools with which to solve problems, build relationships, and generate new ideas. Your thinking will be improved by new stimuli, whether the source is people, books, courses, conversations, or experiences. Exposure to new ideas in any form will keep you sharp and help you stay creative. In this section, I offer up some of the habits I've observed in my most learning-hungry clients and give a few suggestions for making ongoing learning part of your regular routine.

71. Daily News

I read key sections of the paper (online or hard copy) daily and am able to converse on at least a basic level about current events and world issues.

There's an expectation that those in leadership roles have some sense of the world beyond the end of their nose. And, given the ambassadorial role of business leaders, you'll often find yourself in situations where you will have to converse with people of different backgrounds and interests. So it's practical and useful to have some knowledge of what's going on in the larger world. You never want to be the only one at a cocktail party who hasn't heard about something big that happened on the world stage.

In *How to Talk to Anyone, Anytime, Anywhere*, Larry King reveals that his ability to ask great questions comes from being informed. The best way to build an authentic relationship with people is to ask genuinely interested questions about something they're involved in, and you will be better equipped to do this if you have at least a passing knowledge of current events and common topics.

Form some habits that help you stay current. Have the newspaper delivered to your house and read it over breakfast, or spend ten to fifteen minutes reading when you first get to the office. You can read the paper on the subway, use a news app on your mobile device as you ride the commuter train, or listen to an all-news station on your drive to work. News is so accessible that there's no excuse not to have a basic knowledge of the day's events. On the weekends, you can dig a little deeper into subjects and events of particular interest.

72. Reading

I read on a regular basis.

In order to stay abreast of current thinking related to your role and responsibilities, you will find it valuable to create a habit whereby you are consuming new ideas in the areas of leadership, motivation, human behavior, and business thinking regularly. In addition, many leaders I know make a point of reading biographies and histories to understand how great leaders of all sorts thought, behaved, and strategized. Fiction can provide an excellent change of pace from the analytical thinking you do all day long. No matter what you choose, reading helps expand your vocabulary; improve concentration, focus, and reasoning skills; and reduce stress, so take a technology break and learn something new.

I have several CEO clients who consume at least one book a week, as well as Executive Book Summaries (summary.com) or Philosophers' Notes (entheos.com/philosophersnotes) of several others, proving that no matter how busy you are, you can always find time for something that proves itself to be useful and enjoyable.

73. Target Topics

I know the topics that are important to me and I work to stay current with them.

The idea here is focus. Ideas and information are everywhere. Leaders who put themselves in a learning mind-set and constantly expose themselves to new ideas are strengthening their knowledge base, but they are also susceptible to distraction and loss of focus. There's so much to learn and nowhere near enough time to learn it all. You're going to come across fascinating things you want to pursue, but with only so much time in the day you must remain focused on your priorities.

Use a tool like Google Alerts to hone in on five key topics that you want to follow. Subscribe to some podcasts, RSS feeds, and magazines in your chosen topic areas. Don't set your horizons too wide. At some point, an item on your list will cease to be important or useful, and if that happens you can take it off your list—and do be sure to drop an item before you add something new. The things on your list can be a mix of business and personal interests if you like and if you feel you've got sufficient space after the work topics are covered. I know one professional who has three work-related topics on his list, but the other two items are about Broadway, a passion of his.

It's easy to get tempted, and you can lose time really quickly traveling from one topic to another, skimming across the surface like a water bug and never knowing any one thing very well. Skimming is useful if it gives you conversational fodder about a wide variety of things, but be sure you're diving deeply into the priority topics before letting yourself surf across the surface.

74. Current Business Climate

I stay current with issues related to my organization's business and industry.

There will be key things you want to stay on top of. One of my clients is a senior leader in a mining company that has mine sites in several volatile parts of the world. He makes sure to stay current on the political climates in those areas, because local political activities can potentially affect his business. So whether it's stock market movement, politics, or competitor activity (promotions, new product introductions, sales launches, key personnel changes, etc.), there are things that will have potential impact on your business outside of its day-to-day operations, and you should know about them.

Keeping abreast of developments takes effort. The mining executive isn't going to get the latest news about South America unless he makes a point of looking for it. Make the time to stay current, because it is the only way you will learn about certain things that will likely have longer-term impact on your business.

75. Openness to New Ideas

I am open to new ideas and willing to consider alternate points of view. I can be flexible. I don't have to be right all the time. I can evaluate even dubious facts critically and without bias. I listen well.

Open-mindedness is a choice; it's about not being attached to your agenda or your own ideas. Ask yourself: To what degree am I willing to suspend my own agenda or idea to consider something that might be better? To what degree am I genuinely curious about new ideas, and do I seek them out? You're in a leadership role because you have some vision and a sense of how to move forward, but if the only view you ever consider is your own, you will likely not advance as quickly as if you benefited from the synergy that happens when several people contribute to a solution.

Your willingness to embrace the unexpected is directly related to your ability to have fun and to laugh a little bit throughout the day. Avoid keeping your head down with your nose to the grindstone, fiercely committed to the agenda you've got going. You never know when being surprised by something might spark a new idea or just wake you up.

"I push myself, at least weekly, to read something written from a perspective that I significantly disagree with… It opens my mind to other points of view and (hopefully) avoids the opinionated close-mindedness that can

accompany aging. The side benefit is an ever-widening breadth of material to talk about at cocktail and dinner parties."

—David Wright, CEO, Agora Consulting Partners

(agorainc.com)

76. Development Plan

I know what my development areas and Achilles' heels are and have ongoing plans in place to support my growth in these areas.

As leaders, we require self-awareness and the willingness to admit we're not perfect. One of the most important functions a leader plays is that of a role model, so if you know that there's a skill or leadership competency that's less developed in your own leadership tool kit, be transparent about your efforts to improve. This will not only make you a better leader, it will make you a good example to others in your organization. Most people connect more strongly to someone who has humility and admits to some vulnerability. It gives them hope that they will someday get to where you are.

If you're trying to build capacity in the people in your organization, they must be committed to their own development. The best way to build that commitment is to demonstrate it yourself.

One client who brought me in to work with her team originally wasn't going to get involved at all in the coaching process.

When I suggested it would be good for her team to see her taking part, she agreed, if only to be seen as a role model. As it turned out, she experienced enormous benefits in both her professional and personal life. As she wrote in her testimonial for my website, "My staff and family thank you."

77. Continuing Education

I engage in formal learning on a regular basis.

Learning from experts in an environment designed for that purpose will almost always turn up new ideas. Many people say that if they return from a course or conference with just one thing they can use, it was worth attending. Putting yourself in a formal learning environment is only partly about who is standing in the front of the room. It's also about the attendees; you can learn as much from the participants in a learning environment as you can from the curriculum or the speaker.

You don't need to attend learning events often; you just need to understand and appreciate the value of putting yourself in a formal learning environment and doing it regularly. For those at the very senior level, once a year is probably sufficient, as long as you're staying current with your learning and growth through other means as well.

Learning events are different from reading—they provide an entirely different sort of stimulation. You're not in total control of what you're receiving, which gives you the chance to be surprised by new insights. Learning events are also another way to continue to build your network—by virtue of being in the same place, the attendees already have established common ground, which is a great place to start to build a relationship.

78. Complementary Skill Sets

I have members of my team and people in my personal circle who are strong in areas where I am less so, and I listen to and respect them for their expertise.

To ensure that you have a balanced team working around you, include yourself in the assessment of the team's skills. Hire people with different leadership styles and personalities, functional backgrounds, skills, strengths, and areas for development.

It's easiest to hire people who are just like you, but if you do that you're going to have a very unbalanced team. If you're truly committed to your own development, you will find it hugely beneficial to have people around who are strong in areas where you're not, so you can learn from them, not to mention bring valuable diversity to your team.

79. Expert Resources

I seek advice from experts to ensure that I'm making good decisions and choices in areas where I am not expert. I have a team of experts supporting me, including financial planners, lawyers, accountants, personal trainers, and whoever else is relevant to my particular situation. I value advice from good sources.

The curse of the smart person is the ability to do almost anything at least passably well. This ability to know or do most things gets in the way of delegating, and prevents less experienced people from learning and stretching. At its worst, the tendency to do too many things for yourself can result in poor decisions due to lack of knowledge depth. At best, you're spending time doing something that someone else can do at least as well, if not better.

I was once told that if you can find someone to do a task for half or less of your own hourly rate, it's worth hiring the other person. This logic would have you staffing out quite a number of activities you're probably already doing. And there may be money involved! I can speak from my own experience; when I finally found the right combination of bookkeeper and tax accountant for my business, I learned I had missed thousands of dollars of deductions and expenses just because I didn't have the depth of knowledge to file for the full range of allowable deductions.

Even the things you know how to do and do every day can afford a little expert attention every now and then. Almost every golfer I know takes at least one lesson each season, just to have a pro look at his swing and see where he can make some tweaks to get better performance.

80. Mastermind Group

I have a group of people with whom I meet regularly to get and give support for our respective business goals. I trust the members of the group and I am open and transparent with them.

Introduced in Napoleon Hill's 1937 classic *Think and Grow Rich*, the concept of the mastermind group has evolved to become a key component of many successful executives' practice. A mastermind group can be an incredible resource, if constructed and used properly, as it brings the power of several great brains into your business, and equally gives you the opportunity to contribute to others. This process will strengthen your own problem-solving skills and creative thinking. My own mastermind group has provided me with incredible value in numerous ways: committed time away from the day-to-day business to think creatively and strategically, powerful brainstorming, and the unique resources offered up by my group members.

When creating your own mastermind group, keep the number small and look for members who are equally committed to their own personal and business growth. You need to have a high level of trust in those you choose, and, even with that in place, you'll want to have a mutual agreement of confidentiality. Ideally, the members of your group should all be working in slightly different spaces so you're not directly competing, and members should each bring some different perspective, whether that's via their education, technical skills, or experiences.

A well-constructed mastermind group is balanced both in membership and in process, so that each participant derives approximately equal value from it. At the outset, the group needs to decide where and when to meet and for how long, and should design the time so that each member has an opportunity to bring an issue or problem for the group's attention. In a perfect world, each member is giving and receiving relatively equally.

The Bottom Line

With the business and world environment changing at the speed of light, your organization had better be able to learn and adapt quickly. One of the keys to creating a learning organization is for its leaders to be known as learners. Putting some regular and simple practices in place to ensure you're always raising your own bar will keep your development progressing and help you set a good example for those around you.

9

Have Some Fun!

All work and no play...we've all heard the expression. Having a wide variety of interests not only ensures that you'll be able to converse with a wide variety of people, but also helps re-energize you for the work that you spend most of your time doing. You'll be better able to focus on your business if you take a break from it every now and again. Think of it as cross-training for your mind. I've worked with people who had no interests outside of work, and I've worked with those who are immersed in an array of extracurricular activities. The involved ones always seem more vital, more energized, and more in tune with the world around them. Following are what I consider to be the major categories of activity beyond work that can keep you inspired, motivated, and creative, all of which impacts your ability to succeed professionally and makes you a more interesting person outside your business realm.

81. Hobbies

I have interests and/or activities outside of work that energize and inspire me.

Sometimes people's hobbies give us unique insights into their personalities, interests, and value systems that we can't get otherwise. Whether it's the art they collect or create or the games they play, their hobbies give us additional perspective on who they are and what's important to them. Many people think that they need to wait until they retire to have hobbies, but look at it another way. If you don't have any hobbies now, what will you do when you retire? I know people who've gotten to a point where they can dial down in their professional lives and do other things, but they have no idea where to start. They're out of practice because they haven't pursued anything other than work for years.

Sidney, a partner in the accounting firm where he had worked for the better part of thirty-five years, was sixty-three years old when we met, and was going to be retiring at sixty-five. He was very dedicated and took tremendous pride in his professional accomplishments. The first time I walked into his office, however, I was greeted with an opportunity to get to know him in a completely different way when I commented on the beautiful sculpture on his bookshelf. His face lit up and he proceeded to tell me the story of how he had created the piece over hundreds of painstaking hours. In that moment, I understood him as multidimensional person in a way I had not before, and I could see that he had a very well-developed creative side and artistic aesthetic—not your typical accountant.

As Sidney and I discussed his retirement, it became apparent that he had many interests and was excited about pursuing them with the luxury of more time as he reduced his professional commitments. What was particularly interesting, though, was that over time there had become links between his hobbies and his work—he had acquired several clients for his firm as a result of people he'd met through his sculpture classes, charitable efforts, and recreational pursuits.

"Notwithstanding that I had a successful professional practice and was quite active with my wife in many sporting activities, I was seeking more fulfillment and an activity that perhaps I could carry into retirement. Accordingly, about ten years prior to retirement, I registered for a weekly two-and –a-half hour Thursday night stone sculpting course in my neighborhood. This represented a huge leap of faith as I had no artistic talent.

Well, that was twelve years ago and I am now retired and sculpting has become a passion. With more free time available, the Thursday night classes were replaced with two afternoon classes per week, which I eagerly look forward to.

This exposure to sculpting has broadened my artistic appreciation, and, accordingly, art galleries are now included in all our travel itineraries."

—Sidney Kaushansky, Retired Partner, RSM Richter Chamberland (rsmrch.com)

Nobody says that a hobby has to be terribly time consuming. In fact, I strongly suggest choosing hobbies that can be pursued in small bits of time, if possible. Alternatively, choose a pastime that can be pursued on vacations and weekends, and where you've got some control over the schedule, and look forward to increasing its role in your life when you have time later on.

"Cultivate your inner geek with quirky obsessions. It is all too easy to become consumed with our own pursuits of perfection at work that we can lose the perspective of different viewpoints, new avenues, and ultimately the intelligence advantage that comes from diversity. For many top performers, the relentless drive towards the goal to the exclusion of all else is a huge contributor to success. But too much focus can leave us blind and dangerously vulnerable to our own limitations as leaders.

"That's why I let my obsessive mind have other things to 'go at' and become embroiled in. Lately I've been collecting a very specific style of Omega watch from 1970 (I could go into more detail including serial numbers, etc.—but you'd maybe freak out or check out at the level of detail and probably stop reading). While my demon of 'I know everything' is off busy thinking about its nerdy obsession with Swiss watchmaking and being a world expert in this quirky niche, I am free to listen to what others have to say about what really matters in the business.

"Very successful people often have very individual, odd, and obsessive hobbies and collections. It may be because they need a way to placate their need to be the expert, because they know that winning at the bigger projects in life and work needs the ability to take in multiple viewpoints and sometimes relinquish the power of being the 'know it all' at work."
—Mark Bowden, President, TruthPlane
(truthplane.com)

82. Social Activities

I get out and have fun with people not related to work on a regular basis.

Variety in your social activities is the spice of life. If you are always socializing with people who are associated with your business life, you'll find yourself talking about business all the time. In contrast, if you socialize with people outside your business circle, you'll probably learn something new, not to mention offer your loved ones an opportunity to spend time with you outside of business-related settings. Other than that, it's useful to stretch your conversational muscles now and again, and it's easiest to do this with people with whom you don't have the common ground of work.

Meeting new people and talking about new topics can also be a positive thing for your business, as you could be building your network in creative and diverse ways. In addition, the new stimuli will very likely spark creative thinking that can be applied to your business.

83. Romance

I make regular efforts to invest in and sustain the romantic connection with my partner.

Any relationship that is untended won't survive. Admittedly, it's difficult for someone who has a highly demanding leadership role to think about going home and having to work at a relationship. But the fact is that most successful leaders rely pretty heavily on their spouses for support, both personally and professionally, and will attest to the fact that it's easier for them to be who they need to be when they have a supportive partner. But the supportive partner can't—and eventually won't—continue to give you that support unless you also give time and attention to the relationship.

Implementing things like scheduled date nights is always a good idea, but an even better idea is to sit down with your partner to find out what's important to him or her. I had one client who decided that he would try harder at home, and he made a plan to be home in time for dinner a couple of days a week. After a few days of arriving to find the family minivan leaving to get the kids to activities, he finally asked his wife what she wanted. It turned out that all she wanted was for him to commit to not working on the weekends—that was when she wanted his undivided attention. By not asking what was important to her originally, he created a plan that couldn't possibly achieve his goal of spending more time with the family.

There is no one set of rules to follow in this area. The important principle is to not assume that you know what your partner wants. It's better to ask, and then to make your plans based on what you know for sure will make your partner feel appreciated. Make sure you're investing in this area, even though it's hard to do at the end of a long day. A great relationship doesn't just happen, and it can be a tremendous source of joy, not to mention an incredible professional asset.

84. Travel

I have a list of places I want to visit and vacations I want to take.

Often, when I talk to those in a big leadership role about recreational travel, they roll their eyes because the last thing they want to do is get on another plane. The principle here is not that you need to travel, but that if travel is something you want to do, you should make a plan for it so you're not waiting for that elusive *later* to see the parts of the world you'd like to visit.

The other thing to bear in mind is that recreational travel and business travel offer entirely different perspectives on the same place. If you're in a position to take a day either at the beginning or the end of a business trip, do it, even if it's only to investigate the place enough to know whether you want to come back with your partner or your family.

85. Laughter and Play

I laugh, and make others laugh, regularly. I get silly sometimes and I know how to play and have fun—even, occasionally, at work.

There are many benefits of laughter, all of which combat stress. Laughter boosts immunity, lowers stress hormones, and relaxes your muscles. It reduces fear and anxiety and enhances resilience. Even better, if you laugh with someone you form a connection, and social connectivity is good for us.

The fact that laughter is good and useful is supported by science. The "broaden and build" theory of positive emotions, developed by Barbara Fredrickson, posits that the experience of positive emotions contributes to the development of interpersonal skills and emotional resources. It therefore stands to reason that an organization's capacity to handle stress can be enhanced by creating a culture where laughter and fun are integrated into the normal course of business—into the company culture. The most engaging leaders can take a joke, have a good sense of humor, and know how to balance the weightiness of their day-to-day conversations and decisions with a little bit of fun.

86. Affection

The important people in my life know that I care about them, and I am open to receiving affection and/or kindness from those who care about me.

Everyone has a particular type of communication, or "language," that she understands best. For the very important people in your life, their understanding of how important they are to you is directly related whether you speak their language—rather than your own—when expressing affection. Equally important is that you receive expressions of affection from others in the form that works best for you. In *The Five Love Languages*, Dr. Gary Chapman describes five different ways of expressing love and suggests that every person is tuned to one of these languages above the others. Dr. Chapman identifies physical touch, acts of service, quality time, gifts, and words of affirmation as the five different ways to express love.

In my experience working with busy senior executives, I've noticed that, while their hearts are in the right place, their execution often misses the mark—mostly because, in the interest of time, they make an assumption and act on it rather than ask. The flashy, lavish gift, while easy to acquire and dramatic to unveil, is only going to be a good choice for some people. It will completely miss the mark for others, defeating the purpose of the gesture.

On the other hand, some attention to what your loved one responds to and prefers will equip you to communicate with him in the most effective way possible. One client, whose wife had been training for a marathon, gifted her with a week at an exclusive spa resort starting the day after the big race. Another client, whose partner has a major health issue, suggested that the two of them volunteer at a community center that serves people with that same issue. In both of these cases, the gifts were greeted with great appreciation and gratitude, because they reflected loving attention to what mattered to the recipient rather than the giver.

Learning the preferred language of the people you care about will help you communicate your feelings clearly. If you're not sure, ask—better to have a conversation and get it right than guess and get it wrong. And, in return, be sure your loved ones know what language works best for you, so they can enjoy the feeling of getting it really right the next time they want to show you their appreciation.

87. Brain Fitness

I regularly engage in activities that ensure my brain stays active and will remain so as I age.

Several ongoing studies have concluded that, as we age, we can preserve, and even increase, mental acuity by regularly participating in activities that stimulate the brain in particular ways. The Bronx Aging Study, published in *The New England Journal of Medicine* and led by neurologist Dr. Joe Verghese, has followed almost five hundred people for more than twenty years, observing what they actually do in their lives and tracking the relationship between these choices and brain health. The research found that people who participated in mentally stimulating activities, such as interactive games and dancing, four times a week had a 65 to 75 percent higher probability of remaining sharp than those who did not participate in these activities.

The principle is to make sure that you're challenging your brain. If you're in a position of great responsibility and are expected to make weighty decisions and analyze lots of data, it's critically important to stay sharp.

88. Openness to New Experiences

I am willing to broaden my horizons and have tried something new in the last month.

Most people who have a lot of demands on their time have figured out a structure and schedule for their lives that really works. It ensures they get done what they need to get done, and they get to the places they need to be. The downside is that they get so committed to that structure that it's difficult to see beyond it to a possible new interest or opportunity.

Being open to new experiences, even simply trying a new restaurant, makes you a more interesting person and makes spending time with you more relaxing.

89. Spontaneity

I am occasionally willing to abandon my schedule and plan to do something fun.

Many leaders in very demanding roles have been able to succeed and withstand the pressure in part because they live by a strict set of practices and disciplines. Unfortunately, too much of a good thing can get in the way of having a bit of good old-fashioned fun, not to mention developing the adaptability necessary for a very high level of resilience. Life is not always predictable and disciplined. Life gets messy sometimes. In fact, there's a children's television show entitled *The Magic School Bus* that tries to embed the idea of wild abandon early in life. With the call to action, "Take chances! Make mistakes! Get dirty!" the show communicates the idea that the greatest learning experiences occur in the least predictable environments. If everything about your day and your life is neat and tidy, you might miss some opportunities to learn and have fun.

90. Positivity

My days include, on average, at least three times as many positive events and moments as negative ones.

World-renowned positive psychology researcher Dr. Barbara Fredrickson discovered that experiencing emotions in a ratio of three positive emotions to one negative one every day leads people to a tipping point, beyond which they naturally become more resilient and effortlessly achieve what they once could only imagine. In other words, when you typically experience a high level of stress in the course of a normal day, your ability to thrive will depend upon your ability to intentionally add positive energy to your days.

Interpreting an incident or situation as positive is, in fact, a choice. In other words, it's possible to create almost anything as positive—which means that creating a 3:1 positivity ratio is entirely within your control.

The Bottom Line

Having hobbies and interests outside of work can give you the lift you need to offset the stresses of work. A little lightness and play helps you and your team withstand pressure.

If you don't currently have any hobbies or outside interests, reflect on those things you thought you'd do later and consider whether there might be a way to have a little fun with an activity now, even while your time is limited. If you don't have a list for later, try browsing the magazine section in your local bookstore and see what jumps out at you. You might be surprised.

10

Pause and Reflect

Life moves so quickly that without some conscious practices to ensure you are self-aware, on track toward what's important, insulated from the daily noise of life, and learning from your experiences, you could end up in the wrong place at the end of it all. And our ability to improve our performance, our relationships, and our level of life fulfillment is hugely dependent on our ability to learn from mistakes and not repeat them.

Taking the time to reflect on our experiences and redirect our forward movement is key to achieving our goals, both in business and in life. Following are examples of reflective practices that work for many of my executive-level clients. The more of these you can incorporate into your own repertoire of habits, the greater the likelihood you'll manage stress well and stay focused on your goals.

91. Regular Practice

I have a regular spiritual or reflective practice.

The business environment is not often accepting of terms such as "mindfulness" or "meditation," but that doesn't make the practices any less valuable in the business arena than anywhere else. For some, a formal reflective practice is an ingrained part of their lives through church or a spiritual community with regular and structured rituals. For those who do not choose that form of practice, similar benefits can be derived in other ways.

Yoga, journaling, an "unplugged" walk, time spent gazing at something that brings you peace—any regular practice that turns off the normal noise level and gives you a sense of calm can qualify as a reflective discipline. The high ground here, though, is regular meditation.

Neuroscience is just beginning to uncover the power of meditation, showing that it can change the structure and function of the brain to increase attention span, sharpen focus, and improve memory. As a relaxation technique, it can help to reduce stress, enhance creativity, and build emotional intelligence. Various metrics support the benefits of meditation in the workplace—one study showed a 70 percent reduction in employees' days off due to stress over a three-year period following the introduction of a mindfulness course.

Check *Meditation in a New York Minute* by Mark Thornton for ways to incorporate meditation into even the busiest life.

"Here's where it gets brutally difficult for hard-driving execs who are generally quick to master new challenges. Come to the practice expecting nothing beyond committing to sit (or stand or walk). Holding yourself to a standard of instant mastery leads only to instant frustration and attrition. Mindfulness is a practice that both gets easier and reaches deeper over time. In order to get the most from your practice, you need to expect the least."

—Jonathan Fields, author of *Uncertainty*,
founder GoodLifeProject.com
(jonathanfields.com)

92. Gratitude

I am grateful for much in my life, and I take time every day to reflect on that feeling of gratitude. I express gratitude to others.

Explored in depth in the field of positive psychology, most notably by Dr. Martin Seligman, gratitude has been proven to have a substantial and long-lasting impact on happiness. Regularly expressing gratitude has been found to increase life satisfaction and hope, and reduce anxiety and depression.

Both internal reflection on what you're grateful for as well as an outward expression of gratitude to others are important. Writing a list of things you're grateful for at the end of every day helps you focus on positives and can calm your mind before going to bed, which can contribute to better sleep. Outwardly expressing gratitude to other people has a positive impact on both you and on the recipient of your thanks. Implementing a daily practice of recording gratitude also gives the sense of creating more good things in your life. When you know you'll have to write a few items down at the end of the day, you're on the lookout throughout the day for good things to record, whereas normally you might not notice these seemingly trivial moments.

"For the last two years I have adopted 'with gratitude' as my signature line to close out all written communication...I write it out each time as a mini meditation. I swear the practice has changed my life."
—Betsy Peters, CEO, Cambium Enterprises
(cambiumenterprises.com)

93. Daily Planning

I take at least five minutes every day to ensure I am working on the important things.

It is very easy to get swept up in other people's emergencies—often before you even arrive at the office, given the pervasiveness of mobile devices with their instant e-mail and texting capabilities. Your ability to stay focused on the top priorities and ensure your efforts are pointed in the right direction can be improved by a small, simple, daily check-in practice—a few minutes to plan your work before you actually begin doing it. At minimum, five minutes at the beginning of the day to create the list and five minutes at the end to evaluate how you did against your list will help you keep on track. Even better, try Charlie Gilkey's 10/15 Split process at Productive Flourishing (productiveflourishing.com).

94. Weekly Planning

I plan my week at its outset and reflect on its outcomes at the end of it.

This can be two time blocks or one, but it's a critical process. For some, spending a few minutes Sunday night or Monday morning to set goals and organize time for the week gets things off to a strong start, and taking a few minutes before shutting down on Friday to reflect on what actually occurred provides a check on how closely reality aligned with the plan.

For a more intensive practice, Kim Yost, CEO of Art Van Furniture, has implemented what he calls "Schmonday." Every Sunday evening he goes into his home office and withdraws from the rest of the world for several hours. He does his weekly review and plan, but he also checks in on his goals, does his developmental reading, brainstorms and works on new ideas, and reflects on the direction his life and business are taking. He calls this ritual "Schmonday" because, sandwiched between Sunday and Monday, it feels like he gets the benefit of an extra day in the week that others don't enjoy. And if you're wondering how he does it, it's all in the communication and follow-through. He spends time with his family earlier in the day, usually including a major meal at midday, and then he retreats as he's committed to doing—no excuses and no interruptions, and the people around him are aware and supportive. On the occasions when he's traveling or otherwise committed, he'll find at least a bit of time to have that reflective period he has come to rely on so much.

95. Monthly or Quarterly Planning

I step out of my business at least quarterly, if not more frequently, to examine my business and personal goals and ensure everything is on track.

The ability to course correct is dependent on having a point of view about whether you're on track, and you don't know whether you're on track unless you evaluate on a regular basis. Given the pace of change in business, an annual review and planning cycle is unlikely to keep you as nimble and responsive as necessary. Taking time at least quarterly, and perhaps more frequently depending on the market dynamics in your particular space, ensures that you'll have the opportunity to evaluate and redirect if necessary.

Think of the difference between working "in" the business and working "on" the business. It's almost impossible to have a big-picture perspective when you're mired in the day-to-day activities of the business—working "in" it. Stepping out and looking at things from forty thousand feet enables you to see problems and solutions that are probably not visible from the ground.

The same logic holds true for your personal goals. You may work on them every day, but it's hard to know whether you're on track unless you take a step back and check your progress and direction.

96. Yearly Planning

I retreat once a year to reflect on the past year and plan the upcoming year.

If you are leading others, it's critical that you are known for your clarity and ability to set direction—for yourself and for the business. Consider the perspective that you gain by stepping back monthly or quarterly; the annual process offers a further strategic view.

Many thinkers in the strategic planning field are suggesting that annual planning is irrelevant, given the way the pace of change has accelerated, and that business plans need to be examined on a more frequent basis. That is certainly true, however, alignment with strategy and plans for significant change or major goals need to be viewed over an annual horizon. Incorporating a previous year review is particularly useful in any annual planning process because it offers perspective on exactly how much change has really occurred.

Note the two aspects to this item: first, that you plan the year, and second, that you retreat to plan. It is impossible to plan while in the midst of the frenzy of a normal day. And it is important to avoid creating an annual planning process that is arduous and consuming. Rather, create a streamlined, high-level look at where the business is going.

Review your personal goals annually as well, reflecting on your accomplishments of the previous year and setting new goals in the context of your life plan.

97. Personal History Documentation

I have a journal, scrapbook, diary, or other repository for mementos, records, and reflections on the important events in my life.

We all have them—the old photos, the concert ticket stubs, the party invitations, the school awards and athletic acknowledgements—and where are they? If you're like most people, all your mementos are stashed in boxes and drawers throughout your home or in storage somewhere. But what if someone wanted to write your life story? How would the writer get his hands on all of the documentation and how would he make sense of it when he did acquire it all?

Having one place for all your keepsakes ensures you won't lose track of your precious memories, but that repository can also be used as a motivating force. It's like having a collection—once it's started, you're always on the lookout for items to add to it. It's been said that any life worth living is worth documenting, and having a collection of items representing milestones can give you tangible evidence of the progression of your life and the goals you've achieved.

98. Goal Setting

I set goals regularly and have a practice for setting those goals up for success. I have a central repository for my goals and measures, and I have a practice that ensures the information stays current.

The original personal success guru Napoleon Hill is credited with saying, "A goal is a dream with a deadline." Science supports that statement—setting goals increases the chances you'll achieve the things that are important to you, rather than spend your life dreaming but never realizing those dreams.

Goal setting is a science, and worth understanding in depth. When a person has goals, she is focused, creative, and able to celebrate accomplishments because she's got something by which to measure her efforts.

Creating Your Best Life by Caroline Adams Miller is an excellent resource on the how and why of goal setting and its critical relationship to happiness, and includes dozens of tools and practices to help you succeed. There are also numerous goal-setting software programs and websites (check out smart-goalsoftware.com or your100things.com), and there's always the good old-fashioned hardcover journal.

I'm a big fan of the visual reminder, whether it is in the form of a vision board or pictures stuck to your refrigerator. In fact, changing your environment to remind you of your goals is a scientifically proven process known as "priming." Primes can be a powerful stimulant to behavior change. Every one of the hundreds—or even thousands—of visual, olfactory, auditory, and kinesthetic interactions we have over the course of a day has the potential to impact our ability to achieve our goals. Our subconscious mind is always at work, and if you repeatedly stimulate it with reminders of the things that are important to you, you'll be adding greater fuel to your goal achievement fire.

Set big goals, goals that excite you—they are more inspiring than small ones. Make them specific, tangible, and measurable. Tell people what you're up to—few things spur action like knowing someone is watching! Write your goals down and check in on them often—even consider posting them someplace where you'll see them often, so they remain top of mind.

99. Connected Conversation

I have several people in my life with whom I can have deep, connected conversations and I have those kinds of conversations on a regular basis.

I often ask participants in my workshops to describe their most meaningful relationships. The thing I hear about most frequently is the feeling of being really listened to—of being truly "heard." Engaging in a moment with someone you care about, feeling really heard, and experiencing a deep feeling of connection—that can be incredibly energizing.

Unfortunately, when you're in a fast-paced, stressful, results-oriented environment, connected conversation is hard to come by. That's especially true if you're the person to whom others are accountable. Add to those factors the role that technology plays today in reducing the amount of human contact we have, and it's easy to understand why we are becoming increasingly connection-starved.

Making time for connection—making the effort to reach out to someone for a connected conversation—is worth the effort. The positive effects from connecting with others are lasting. While there are many life experiences that have been proven to have little or no long-term impact on our happiness—like winning a lottery or buying a fancy new car—close relationships may be an exception. Called "hedonic adaptation," we are about as happy after a change in circumstance as we were before, in most cases, except when it comes to relationships. We are more likely to continue to want our close relationships, even after we attain them, and to continue to derive positive emotions from them.

100. Intuition

I recognize when my intuition is engaged, and I value and reflect upon the messages it sends me.

The best business leaders I've met all acknowledge a sixth sense or instinct that guides them. They willingly accumulate the same data that everyone else has, and then allow their extra sense to help guide them toward a decision. Intuition is intensely individual and can take any number of forms, but it is an important tool for anyone faced with big decisions on a regular basis. Not that the value of data should ever be diminished—far from it—but when the facts are murky or the data conflicts, intuition has proven for many to be a powerful guide.

Intuition is usually aligned with values. Think of a time when you felt conflicted or concerned about a particular decision or course of action but couldn't specify the source of your problem. You may have had a vague sense of foreboding or fear but were not able to explain it. That's an example of a situation where your brain is trying to override the messages coming from the other decision-influencing centers in your body (which are different for everyone). So next time you're faced with a big decision where the course forward is not perfectly clear, take a moment and check to see what sensations you're experiencing—your intuition may be trying to send you a message.

"The intellect has little to do on the road to discovery. There comes a leap in consciousness, call it intuition or what you will, and the solution comes to you and you don't know how or why."
—Albert Einstein, Theoretical Physicist

The Bottom Line

Regular reflection and planning practices, although at odds with the pace and interaction style of our world these days, provide the foundation for well-directed, intentional accomplishment. Reflection ensures that you learn from and stay respectful of past experiences while supporting forward movement that has a higher probability of getting you where you want to go. While this set of practices shows last in our model, the items reflected here have the greatest potential for impact on the quality of your leadership and your life. If you already practice many of these habits, keep up everything you're doing and work toward being able to do all the items. If none are familiar, start small and work toward incorporating all ten.

AFTERWORD

One hundred things to do. One hundred practices. Are you overwhelmed? Or are you purposeful, focused, and taking action? Are you an 85, confident and strategic in your efforts to continually raise your game? Or are you a 31, early on in your work of becoming a leader with a new understanding of what it will take to be successful—and healthy—and happy?

The ten areas of focus and the respective 100-point system highlighted in *The Complete Executive* reflect the areas of effort and practice that, in my experience of working with senior executives for over sixteen years, have the greatest impact on performance. As I mentioned at the outset, the system I describe here is comprehensive but not all-encompassing, however it does represent an overview of the kinds of disciplines that can make a material difference to a leader's ability to thrive at the top.

I invite you to take the assessment, either in the Appendix or at karenwrightcoaching.com, and determine which of the ten chapters represents your area of greatest development opportunity. Work on the items in that section until you're comfortable that you're making progress, and then move to one of your other lower scoring areas. Work the program continually, either on your own, with a study group, or with a coach, to make consistent progress towards achieving a score greater than 80. Once you achieve a score of 80 or greater, re-take the assessment from the beginning to see whether your standards have changed—oftentimes, as the development work progresses, what qualified as sufficient early on is not so later.

No matter what your score or how far you take your efforts to develop with the system, I promise you'll find that introducing some of the habits into your life will contribute to your feeling calmer, more grounded and centered, and more able to withstand the extraordinary demands of leadership at the very top. My best to you on your journey.

The Complete Executive Assessment

The Complete Executive

The 10-Step System for Great Leadership Performance

Focus	#	Practice	Ideal State	0	.5	1
Make Health and Fitness Your Top Priority	1	Disciplined eating habits and a clear personal philosophy about food	I know how to eat (what, when, how much, how often) to fully energize myself and support my long-term health. I am able to resist the temptations and deal with the meal irregularities that occur related to my work schedule and demands.			
	2	Daily Activity and Energy Awareness	I break a sweat and/or walk 10,000 steps every day. I know what time of day best suits me for exercise and I plan the rest of my day around it. I make accommodations and adjustments to my routine when my work schedule interferes with my normal exercise practices.			
	3	Weight management	I maintain a healthy weight.			
	4	Goals and Metrics	I have goals for my health stats and fitness efforts, and I track against those metrics on a regular and ongoing basis.			
	5	Hydration and Supplementation.	I drink water several times a day and I support my health with vitamins and supplements to ensure I stay vital and fully energized.			

6 Cross-training and recovery strategies — I have changed my exercise routine in the past three months and I have at least three different types of exercise I enjoy and pursue regularly. I warm up before and cool down after exercise.

7 Sleep — I know how much sleep I require in order to function well and I get that amount most nights. I get up early, feeling rested and energized.

8 Diagnostics — I have had a physical examination in the last year and am up to date on all key diagnostic tests, including those related to age. I follow all professionally recommended protocols to manage any current and/or chronic conditions I have.

9 Support mechanisms and equipment — Every item I require in order to function optimally (eyeglasses, orthotics, hearing aids, etc.) is up to date and working well. Everything I need for my exercise activities is functional, up to date, accessible and clean.

10 Social support — I have exercise partners, group members or other accountability and sociability partners specifically related to exercise, and I ask them to call me out if they notice I am faltering in my commitments to exercise.

Total

Focus		Practice	Ideal State	0	.5	1
Craft a Life Plan	11	Goal alignment with partner	My spouse/life partner and I have discussed our individual and shared long-term goals. We know where we're going and how we're going to get there together.			
	12	Financial plan	I have calculated my long-term financial requirements and I am living based on a plan to meet those requirements.			
	13	Career Goal	I know what I want to achieve in my career and I have a plan to accomplish my goals.			
	14	Mentors/coaches	I have people I can – and do – turn to for advice and support.			
	15	Retirement lifestyle vision	I have thought about how I want to be living my life 10, 20, and 30 years from now and I have a plan for achieving that vision.			
	16	Social service/ contribution	I know which causes and issues are important to me and I make contributions of money and/or time to organizations that support those causes and issues.			
	17	Legacy/significance	I know the impact I want to have on the world or my chosen segment of it, and my career and personal plans will support me in creating that impact.			
	18	Residence/ geography	I live in a part of the world that I enjoy and my home provides me with necessary peace and restful sanctuary.			
	19	Perfect days	My days energize me and provide opportunities for me to work in "flow."			
	20	Will and bequests	My will and power of attorney documents are up to date and include bequests to charitable or cause-based organizations that do work I believe in.			
Total						

Focus		Practice	Ideal State	0	.5	1
Invest in Relationships	21	Primary	I have a life partner and we are both happy in our relationship OR we are actively involved in a process to strengthen our relationship OR I am single and happy.			
	22	Children	I am happy with, and make regular investments in, my relationships with my children – OR I have no children and accept that status.			
	23	Extended family	I have amicable relationships with my extended family and have no bad blood or unfinished business to clean up.			
	24	Neighbors	I know my neighbors by name and have chatted with some of them recently.			
	25	Community	I feel like I am part of a community outside of work.			
	26	Competitors	I have amicable professional relationships with key players at my major competitors.			
	27	Peers	I have same-level friends and colleagues and regularly invest in my relationships with them.			
	28	Direct Reports	I know something about my direct reports and their lives outside of work.			
	29	Friends	I have a number of friends who've been in my life for a long time and who know they're very valuable to me even if we don't see each other often.			
	30	Board of Directors	I connect regularly with every member of my Board and work to foster positive, transparent relationships with each of them.			
Total						

Focus		Practice	Ideal State	0	.5	1
Be a Real Leader	31	Leadership Philosophy	I have a clear philosophy about and approach to leadership and conduct myself according to that philosophy.			
	32	Performance Review and 360 Feedback	I have had a 360 degree feedback survey (qualitative or quantitative) in the past two years AND have acted upon the feedback I received. I have had a performance review in the past year.			
	33	Values and Walking the Talk	I live and lead by a clear set of personal values and I want to be challenged if my behavior communicates something different from those values.			
	34	Core Competencies	I operate at least capably if not masterfully, across all the core competencies identified in our organization's leadership model. I know where my areas of development are and am taking action to constantly improve.			
	35	"Soft" Skills	I understand that how I get things done is at least as important as what gets accomplished. I know when to coach and when to direct, when to influence and how to inspire. I am an ongoing student of leadership and constantly seek examples and role models. I listen well and know how to both give and receive feedback constructively.			

36 Performance and Conduct Expectations	The people in my organization know what is expected of them and what the implications are of not meeting those expectations. We have a communications program in place to ensure expectations are clear to everyone at every level and training/education support is available where necessary.
37 Innovation and Creativity	I believe that relevant innovation is critical to our success. I welcome new ideas and embrace a climate where creativity is valued and encouraged. I believe failure is an opportunity to learn.
38 Synthesis	I can see patterns and systems in apparently disparate sets of information. I can connect the dots and lead the development of long-term, big-picture solutions.
39 Presentation and Communication Skills	I manage my appearance and work style to ensure I am setting the desired tone for others in my organization. I work continuously to hone my written and verbal communication skills to ensure I am clear and compelling at all times. I am comfortable with public speaking.
40 Personal Story	I know how to tell my personal success story in a way that aligns with my leadership brand and reflects my personal values.

Total

Focus	Practice		Ideal State	0	.5	1
Put the Business Basics in Place	41	Vision	My organization or team has a clear vision for the long-term impact we are striving to make, and every employee knows and understands the vision.			
	42	Mission	My organization or team knows what we're good at and and how we will work to advance our vision. Each employee understands how they can contribute.			
	43	Strategic Plan	My organization or team has a strategic plan and we review it annually.			
	44	Five Year Targets and Goals	We have metrics in place to measure our growth and success five years into the future and we examine those metrics annually and revise as appropriate. We do not react to short term aberrations in the marketplace			
	45	One-year Operating Plan	My organization or team has a one-year operating plan and we have the resources in place to execute against that plan.			
	46	Talent Review and Succession Plan	My organization or team has annual talent reviews and has successors identified—and prepared—for all key positions, including my own. We value, and seek, diversity across our entire workforce.			

47	Measures of Success	My organization or team knows, and measures, the factors beyond the financial goals that will ensure we stay on track toward our objectives.	
48	Crisis Management Plan	My organization or team has a formal plan in place to deal with emergencies and unforeseen events, both internal and external to the company.	
49	Corporate Social Responsibility Plan	My organization or team has a clear point of view on issues that we support and we have programs in place to support those causes.	
50	Technology Plan	My organization has a plan to ensure we stay current and effective in our use of technology to support our business, both internally and externally. We understand how to apply technology to support productivity, process and systems management, customer connections, and employee recruitment/retention.	
Total			

Focus	Practice	Ideal State	0	.5	1
Take Charge of Your Career	51 Career plan	I am clear about what I need to accomplish in order to feel that I have been successful in my career, and I have short and medium term goals that are part of that plan. I have set approximate timing milestones for each key goal.			
	52 Personal/ Professional Goal Alignment	My career plan aligns with and contributes to my overall personal life plan.			
	53 Passion for the Business	I believe in my organization's mission and vision and I am passionate about the business we're in. I am my company's best salesperson.			
	54 Resumé	I have an up-to-date resumé.			
	55 Salary and Market Value	I am comfortable with my compensation and know where I stand in the external marketplace based on my role, organization, industry, and location.			
	56 Recruiter Connections	I know who the major recruiters are in my area, by both functional and sector specialty and I have connections to all of them.			

57	Lessons from Adversity	I have reflected on the challenges I've encountered along my professional journey and I understand the learning opportunity embedded in each of those challenges.
58	"Elevator Speech"	I have a summary statement about who I am professionally and can distinguish that from what I do.
59	Skills Inventory	I know what I'm good at and am able to comfortably discuss my strengths.
60	Role Models	I know which companies and/or leaders I respect and who I'd like to learn from in the future.

Total

Focus		Practice	Ideal State	0	.5	1
Build a Valuable Network	61	Tools	I've got an active, up-to-date LinkedIn profile. I understand and have evaluated Twitter's usefulness to my network-building efforts. I am aware of and use the other connection tools common in my professional arena.			
	62	Alumni Association	I belong to the alumni association from my alma mater and keep my contact information up to date with them.			
	63	Professional Groups	I am an active member of my professional association.			
	64	Lunches/casual meetings	I have a schedule of regular breakfast/lunch/coffee meetings that keep me connected with people outside my immediate circle of peers, friends and colleagues.			
	65	Introductions and Recommendations	I have clear criteria to use when I receive requests to use my network to assist others.			
	66	Responsiveness to requests	I have a clear criteria regarding how and to whom I will respond when I receive requests for my time or connections.			

67	Requests for Information or Resources	I reach out into my network if I need information or connection to a resource or person.		
68	Maintenance	I have a process for connecting into my network on a regular basis.		
69	Club memberships	I know which local private clubs are the best to belong to such that I have the opportunity to meet useful contacts with common interests.		
70	Network Management	I know which companies, skill sets, knowledge bases and individuals I want in my network and I have a plan to expand it to include them. I examine my network regularly and have a process for weeding out people who are no longer relevant or desirable.		
Total				

Focus	Practice	Ideal State	0	.5	1
Be a Lifelong Learner	71 Daily news	I read key sections of the newspaper (online or hard copy) and am able to converse on at least a basic level about current events and world issues.			
	72 Reading	I read on a regular basis.			
	73 Target topics	I know the topics that are important to me and I work to stay current with them.			
	74 Current business climate	I stay current with issues related to my organization's business and industry.			
	75 Openness to new ideas	I am open to new ideas, and willing to consider alternate points of view. I can be flexible. I don't have to be right all the time. I can evaluate even dubious facts critically and without bias. I listen well.			
	76 Development plan	I know what my development areas and Achilles' heels are and have ongoing plans in place to support my growth in these areas.			

77	Continuing education	I engage in formal learning on a regular basis.
78	Complementary skill sets	I have members of my team and people in my personal circle who are strong in areas where I am less so, and I listen to and respect them for their expertise.
79	Expert resources	I seek advice from experts to ensure I'm making good decisions and choices in areas where I am not expert. I have a team of experts supporting me, including financial planners, lawyers, accountants, personal trainers and whoever else is relevant to my particular situation. I value advice from good sources.
80	Mastermind group	I have a group of people with whom I meet regularly to get and give support for our respective business goals. I trust the members of the group and I am open and transparent with them.

Total

Focus	Practice	Ideal State	0	.5	1
Have Some Fun!	81 Hobbies	I have interests and/or activities outside of work that energize and inspire me.			
	82 Social activities	I get out and have fun with non-work-related people on a regular basis.			
	83 Romance	I make regular efforts to invest in and sustain the romantic connection with my partner.			
	84 Travel	I have a list of places I want to visit and vacations I want to take.			
	85 Laughter and play	I laugh, and make others laugh, regularly. I get silly sometimes and I know how to play and have fun – even, occasionally, at work.			
	86 Affection	The important people in my life know that I care about them and I am open to receiving affection and/or kindnesses from those who care about me.			
	87 Brain Fitness	I regularly engage in activities that ensure my brain stays sharp and will remain so as I age.			
	88 Openness to new experiences	I am willing to broaden my horizons and have tried something new in the last month.			
	89 Spontaneity	I am occasionally willing to abandon my schedule and do something fun.			
	90 Positivity	My days include, on average, at least three times as many positive events and moments as negative ones.			
Total					

Focus		Practice	Ideal State	0	.5	1
Pause and Reflect	91	Regular practice	I have a regular spiritual or reflective practice.			
	92	Gratitude	I am grateful for much in my life, and I take time every day to reflect on that feeling of gratitude. I express gratitude to others.			
	93	Daily planning	I take at least five minutes every day to ensure I'm working on the important things.			
	94	Weekly planning	I plan my week at its outset and reflect on its outcomes at the end of it.			
	95	Monthly or quarterly planning	I step out of my business at least quarterly, if not more frequently, to examine the business and personal goals to ensure everything is on track.			
	96	Yearly planning	I retreat once a year to reflect on the past year and plan the upcoming year.			
	97	Personal history documentation	I have a journal, scrapbook, diary or other repository for mementos, records and reflections on the important events in my life.			
	98	Goal setting	I set goals regularly and have a practice for setting those goals up for success. I have a central repository for my goals and measures, and I have a practice that ensures the information stays current.			
	99	Connected conversation	I have several people in my life with whom I can have deep, connected conversations AND I do so on a regular basis.			
	100	Intuition	I recognize when my intuition is engaged and I value and reflect upon the messages it sends me.			
Total						

Scoring Summary

Focus Area	Starting Score	3 months	6 months	9 months	12 months
Make Health and Fitness Your Top Priority					
Craft a Life Plan					
Invest in Relationships					
Be a Real Leader					
Put the Business Basics in Place					
Take Charge of Your Career					
Build a Valuable Network					
Be a Lifelong Learner					
Have Some Fun!					
Pause and Reflect					
Total					

BIBLIOGRAPHY

Amabile, Teresa, and Steven Kramer. "How Leaders Kill Meaning at Work." *McKinsey Quarterly*, January 2012.

Buckingham, Marcus. *Go Put Your Strengths to Work: 6 Powerful Steps to Achieve Outstanding Performance*. Free Press, 2010.

Buckingham, Marcus, and Donald Clifton. *Now Discover Your Strengths*. Free Press, 2001.

Covey, Stephen R. *The 7 Habits of Highly Effective People*. Free Press, 2004.

Csikszentmihalyi, Mihaly. *Flow: The Psychology of Optimal Experience*. Harper Perennial, 1991.

Cullen, Lisa Takeuchi. "How to Get Smarter, One Breath at a Time." *Time Magazine*, January 10, 2006.

DePaulo, Bella. *Singled Out: How Singles Are Stereotyped, Stigmatized and Ignored and Still Live Happily Ever After*. New York: St. Martin's Griffin, 2007.

Diener, Ed, and Robert Biswas-Diener. *Happiness: Unlocking the Mysteries of Psychological Wealth*. Wiley-Blackwell, 2008.

Ferrazzi, Keith. *Never Eat Alone: And Other Secrets to Success, One Relationship at at Time*. Crown Business, 2005.

Fox, Justin. "The Economics of Well-Being." *Harvard Business Review*, January–February 2012.

Fredrickson, Barbara. "What Good Are Positive Emotions?" *Review of General Psychology*, 2:3 (1998): 300–319.

Fredrickson, Barbara L. *Positivity: Groundbreaking Research Reveals How to Embrace the Hidden Strength of Positive Emotions, Overcome Negativity, and Thrive*. Crown Archetype, 2009.

Hauri, Peter, and Shirley Lynde. *No More Sleepless Nights, Revised Edition*. Wiley, 1996.

Hill, Napoleon. *Think and Grow Rich.* Ballantine Books, 1987.

Hsieh, Tony. *Delivering Happiness: A Path to Profits, Passion, and Purpose.* Business Plus, 2010.

Kabat-Zinn, Jon. *Full Catastrophe Living: Using the Wisdom of Your Body and Mind to Face Stress, Pain, and Illness.* Delta, 1990.

Kimsey-House, Karen, Henry Kimsey-House, and Phillip Sandahl. *Co-Active Coaching: Changing Business, Transforming Lives,* Third Edition. Boston: Nicholas Brealey Publishing, 2011.

Kirby, Julia, and Christopher Meyer. "Runaway Capitalism." *Harvard Business Review,* January–February 2012.

Klinenberg, Eric. *Going Solo: The Extraordinary Rise and Surprising Appeal of Living Alone.* New York: Penguin Press HC, 2012.

Miller, Caroline Adams. *Creating your Best Life.* New York: Sterling Publishing, 2009.

Nour, David. *Relationship Economics: Transform your Most Valuable Business Contacts into Personal and Professional Success.* Wiley, 2011.

Pink, Daniel. *Drive: The Surprising Truth About What Motivates Us.* Riverhead Hardcover, 2009.

Rosenthal, Joshua. *Integrative Nutrition.* New York: Integrative Nutrition Publishing, 2008.

Rutledge, Pamela Brown. "Social Networks: What Maslow Misses." *Psychology Today,* November 8, 2011.

Seligman, Martin. *Authentic Happiness: Using the New Positive Psychology to Realize Your Potential for Lasting Fulfillment.* Free Press, 2002.

Spreitzer, Gretchen, and Christine Porath. "Creating Sustainable Performance." *Harvard Business Review,* January–February 2012.

Thornton, Mark. (2006). *Meditation in a New York Minute: Super Calm for the Super Busy.* Sounds True, Incorporated.

Turner, Natasha. *The Hormone Diet.* Rodale Books, 2011.

Verghese, Joe, Richard B. Lipton, Mindy J. Katz, Charles B. Hall, Carol A. Derby, Gail Kuslansky, Anne F. Ambrose, Martin Sliwinski, and Herman Buschke. "Leisure Activities and the Risk of Dementia in the Elderly." *New England Journal of Medicine* 348 (2003): 2508–2516.

Yost, Kim. *Pumptitude: 68 Ways to Make a Great Life.* 2011.

ACKNOWLEDGMENTS

I'm sure every first-time author gets to this stage in the process and finds it harder than they imagined. Even though *The Complete Executive* represents a distillation of sixteen years of professional experience, it would not have come to pass if not for the influences and learning that occurred in the lifetime prior, so the idea of selecting just a few people for acknowledgment feels less than appropriate because I have learned so much from so many. That said, following is an attempt to thank those who have been particularly supportive and influential throughout this process.

Working with the team at Bibliomotion has been a dream. Erika Heilman, Jill Friedlander, and Susanna Kellogg, you've been firm but fair, open to suggestions, clear when your way really needed to be the way, and willing to listen to the occasional panic attack. Your extended team of project manager Jill Schoenhaut, Shelton Interactive, and Cave Henricks have been knowledgeable, creative, and very patient with me as I learned the ropes. Thanks for making this experience really fun and rich with learning. You're creating a new publishing model and I know you are going to be brilliantly successful with it.

The book would never have gotten out of my head and into

its current form if not for the wisdom, counsel, and occasional not-so-gentle nudging of Michael Bungay Stanier. You are an esteemed colleague and treasured friend, not to mention icon of style, and I am so glad that, after circling each other for years in the coaching community, you finally suggested that we meet.

Every coach should have a coach, and I've had many over the years. While each has had their impact, Caroline Adams Miller stands apart, and not just because she had the guts to be photographed beside an inflatable Hallowe'en snow globe for use in a professional publication. Caroline, thanks for showing how science and positive psychology can make coaching more powerful, and for challenging me to follow through on what I said was important.

I've been a proud member of the professional coaching community almost since its inception, and I've had the pleasure and privilege along the way to learn from and collaborate with many of the best. Thomas Leonard and Coach U were the source of the original 100-point systems and the coach training programs that propelled me into the career—and life—of my dreams. Bobette, Donna, and Guy—you created Conversation Among Masters to bring the best of the best together every year and, while I can't always be there in person I always know that there's a community of practice that I call home.

Many of my clients are represented in *The Complete Executive*, whether by name or by story, and I thank you all for the privilege of working in such close relationship with you. You are all an ongoing source of inspiration and learning for me, and you are the reason I love my work.

Jonathan Fields and the Good Life Project. In just a few short months you have become an important tribe for me, one I hope will remain so for the rest of my life. Jennifer, Cynthia, Angela, Kelly, Karen, Ashley, Betsy, Margy, Linda, Eric, Kristoffer, Brendon, Max and Chris—you are wise and brilliant and generous and you are all changing the world in important ways. I feel privileged to know you and benefit from your advice and support, both personally and professionally. And Jonathan, thank you for creating the tribe and for being a personal mentor and guide to me—I am grateful for your support.

Martha Campbell is that rare treasure—a lifetime friend. You're a great lawyer and a brilliant artist, but most importantly you are the kindest, most generous person I know. You've been there for me through thick and thin since the first day of high school and you are a rock in the chaotic waters of my life. Thank you.

My brother, Dave Wright—thank you for your eagle editing eye and early enthusiasm for the concepts in the book. Your help was invaluable.

Brendan and Conor—you're strong, smart, resilient, creative young men and I'm incredibly proud of you. Thanks for your suggestions when I was stressed and overwhelmed, and for eating slightly more pizza than might have been best during the final stages of my writing. I'm the luckiest mother in the world.

ABOUT THE AUTHOR

Karen Wright is a student of human behavior. Through her career in consumer packaged goods marketing and advertising she became fascinated with understanding why people do what they do. The emergence of the field of professional coaching provided a perfect platform for taking that fascination to a deeper level in support of people who are truly committed to their own growth and development. She is the owner of a coaching company, Parachute Executive Coaching, based in Toronto, Canada, and leads a team of coaches who work to build leadership capacity at the senior levels of large organizations across North America. Karen's own coaching focuses on working with executives to achieve the elusive combination of health, happiness and success.

Karen has an MBA from the Ivey School at Western University in London, Ontario, Canada, and has studied coaching skills extensively through the completion of two accredited training programs as well as participation in Dr. Martin Seligman's first Positive Psychology coach training course and a certification as a Health Coach through the Institute of Integrative Nutrition. One of the first Professional Certified Coaches in Canada and now one of an elite group of Master Certified Coaches globally, Karen is a leader in the coaching profession.

Karen lives in Toronto, Canada with her two sons.

WHAT'S NEXT?

If you have enjoyed *The Complete Executive*, I invite you to work the program and stay connected with me so I can help you unleash all of your leadership and personal power. There are several ways to do that:

Take the online version of the assessment and learn about the self-guided, individual and group coaching programs:
    www.karenwrightcoaching.com

Connect with me:
    On Twitter: @karenwright1
    On LinkedIn: http://ca.linkedin.com/in/karenwrightcoach
    On Facebook: www.facebook.com/karenwrightcoaching

Work with members of my coaching team:
    www.parachuteexecutivecoaching.com

Share your experiences and stories as you work The Complete Executive system:
    stories@karenwrightcoaching.com

Invite me to speak to your organization or group:
speaking@karenwrightcoaching.com

Every step you take, every habit you adopt, and every practice you add to your repertoire brings you that much closer to being The Complete Executive. I look forward to hearing your success stories!

K.